THE HOUSE BOAT BOYS

OR, DRIFTING DOWN TO THE SUNNY SOUTH

I0616940

ST. GEORGE RATHBORNE

1st WORLD
LIBRARY
Literary Society

The House Boat Boys

St. George Rathborne

© 1st World Library, 2009
PO Box 2211
Fairfield, IA 52556
www.1stworldlibrary.com
First Edition

LCCN: 2009923503

Softcover ISBN: 978-1-4218-8884-2
Hardcover ISBN: 978-1-4218-8983-2
eBook ISBN: 978-1-4218-8785-2

Purchase *"The House Boat Boys"*
as a traditional bound book at:
www.1stWorldLibrary.com/purchase.asp?ISBN=978-1-4218-8884-2

1st World Library is a literary, educational organization
dedicated to:

- Creating a free internet library of downloadable ebooks

- Hosting writing competitions and offering book publishing
  scholarships.

Interested in more 1st World Library books? contact:
literacy@1stworldlibrary.com
Check us out at: www.1stworldlibrary.com

1ˢᵗ World Library Literary Society

Giving Back to the World

"If you want to work on the core problem, it's early school literacy."

- James Barksdale, former CEO of Netscape

"No skill is more crucial to the future of a child, or to a democratic and prosperous society, than literacy."

- Los Angeles Times

"Literacy... means far more than learning how to read and write... The aim is to transmit... knowledge and promote social participation."

- UNESCO

"Literacy is not a luxury, it is a right and a responsibility. If our world is to meet the challenges of the twenty-first century we must harness the energy and creativity of all our citizens."

- President Bill Clinton

"Parents should be encouraged to read to their children, and teachers should be equipped with all available techniques for teaching literacy, so the varying needs and capacities of individual kids can be taken into account."

- Hugh Mackay

CHAPTER I

WHAT A LETTER FROM A TRAMP STEAMER DID

"I say, what's gone wrong now, Maurice, old fel?"

The speaker, a roughly clad boy of about fifteen or over, caught hold of his companion's sleeve and looked sympathetically in his face.

The lad whom he called Maurice was better dressed, and he seemed to carry with him a certain air of refinement that was lacking in his friend, who was of a rougher nature. Despite this difference he and Thad Tucker were the closest of chums, sharing each other's joys and disappointments, small though they might be.

They had met just now at the post-office of a little country town not many miles below Evansville, Indiana, as the afternoon mail was being sorted.

The yellow flood of the great Ohio River could be seen from where they stood, glowing in the early November sunshine.

Upon being greeted with these words Maurice Pemberton shook his head dolefully.

"It's come, just as I've been half expecting it these four months, Thad. The old couple I live with have sold their house and leave for Chicago in a week. That turns me out into the Streets, for you know they've given me a home ever since mother, who was a friend of Mrs. Jasper, died; and in return I've tried to make good by doing all their gardening and other work between school hours. Now a son has sent for them to come and make their home with him. Pretty tough on a fellow not to know where he's going to sleep after a single week."

But Thad was smiling now, as though an idea had flashed into his head that gave him reason for something akin to pleasure.

"Well, I don't know; if it comes to the worst, Pard Maurice, you're a dozen times welcome to share my old bunky on the shanty- boat. I'd just love to make another cot like mine, and have you there. Say, wouldn't it be grand? Of course, though, you'd find it a pretty poor contraption alongside the house you've lived in; but if it was a thousand dollar launch still you'd be just as welcome, and you know it," he said with a heartiness that could not be misunderstood.

The other looked at him affectionately, and was about to say something in return when the window of the post-office was thrown open as a signal that the mail had been distributed. So Maurice stepped up to secure the usual papers, together with an occasional letter, that came for the Jaspers.

Thad saw him start and look curiously at one letter, and then begin to tear the end off as though it were meant for him.

Watching curiously, all unaware how history was making at that identical moment for himself and Maurice, he saw the other smile and nod his head, while an expression of delight

St. George Rathborne

gradually crept over his face.

Then Maurice remembered that his chum was standing there waiting for him to come, and together they passed out of the little office.

"If that doesn't beat the Dutch!" Maurice was saying, half to himself, as he looked at the letter he was holding in a hand that trembled a little despite his efforts to seem composed.

"It cert does," declared Thad, positively; and then both laughed.

"Excuse me, old fellow, for not speaking up and letting you into the facts; but you can see for yourself that the thing's kind of staggering me a bit. Just to think of its coming today of all times, when I'm most in need of a home. Talk to me about chance; I guess there's something better than accident about this."

"All right; I agree with you, Pard Maurice; but suppose you let a little light in on my dumb brain. Where's the letter from, and what does she say?" observed the other, eyeing the envelope dubiously, for he had a sudden fear that it meant the sundering of the ties that bound them together.

"New Orleans, and it comes from Uncle Ambrose—you've often heard me speak of him, and that he was a captain on a tramp steamer that went all over the world picking up cargoes. For three years I've lost track of him, but he hasn't quite forgotten his nephew Maurice it seems. Listen to what he says, after telling me how he's beginning to feel lonely without a relative near, and growing old all the time. Sit down here where we can look out on the bully old river, while I read."

Thad dropped beside him on a stone, and cuddled his arms around his knees in a favorite attitude of his, while he prepared to listen.

"We are billed to be back here in New Orleans about the fifteenth of February, and if you can make it, my boy, I'd like to see you here then. I've got a berth as supercargo open to you, and there's a fine chance to see something of the world; for in the course of three years we are apt to visit the seven seas, and many strange countries. Be sure and come if you care to take up with your old uncle. The older I grow the stronger the ties that bind to the past appeal to me, and it will make me happier to have one of my own blood aboard to share my travels. From your affectionate uncle.

AMBBOSE HADDON.

"On board the Campertown.

"Bully! That's just fine for you, Maurice; but don't you think the captain forgot one thing?" declared Thad.

"What's that?" asked his friend, looking puzzled.

"Why didn't he think to enclose the price of a ticket from here to New Orleans? He might have known money didn't grow on bushes around here."

Maurice laughed.

"I always heard Uncle Ambrose was forgetful of small things, and I guess it's true. Never once entered his head when he was writing. Perhaps it may later, and he'll think to enclose the money from some foreign port. Why, would you believe it, he didn't even mention where the steamer was going to next; only remarked that they sailed in a day or so.

But the tone of the letter is warm, and—why, of course I must accept the invitation. It just seems to come in now at the one time I need it most. You wouldn't want me to let it pass, would you, Thad?"

"I should say not, even if it does hurt some to think of you going away and me staying in this bum old place," said his friend, quickly giving Maurice an affectionate look that spoke volumes.

"If I could only go, too. I'm dead sure uncle would be glad to have you with me on board; and think of the glorious times we could have. Why, it seems too good to be true, doesn't it?"

"I guess it does for me. I'd like to go the worst kind, but where would I pick up the money to pay my way? Of course I might float down the Mississippi on the Tramp all right, given time enough; but that would be kind of lonely business for one; now if you could only—say, I wonder—oh, bosh, of course you wouldn't want to even think of it," and he dropped his head dejectedly.

"Wouldn't think of what? Why don't you go on and finish? You've got some sort of a fine scheme in your head, so explain," demanded Maurice, quickly.

"I was just thinking, that's all, what a great time we might have if we did start out in my little bum boat to make New Orleans. There's three months ahead of us, and scores of shanty-boats float down from Cincinnati to Orleans every fall and winter—you know that. Gee! what fun we could have!" and the two boys started at each other for half a dozen seconds without saying a word; but those looks were more eloquent than all the language ever uttered.

Then Maurice thrust out his hand impulsively.

"Shake! Do you really think we could do it, Thad?" he exclaimed.

"Do I? Why, it would be as easy as pie. Think of it; all you have to do is to let the current carry you along. It's a snap, that's what!" cried the other, brimming over with enthusiasm.

Ah! Thad was yet to learn that a thousand unforeseen difficulties lay in wait for those floating craft that drifted down the great water highway every winter; but "in the bright lexicon of youth there is no such word as fail," and to his eyes the enterprise was a veritable voyage of pleasure, nothing less.

"Then we'll go!" declared Maurice, with vim, shaking his chum's hand furiously. "Given a week to get my traps together, sell what I don't want, lay in some provisions, buy a few things, like a flannel shirt and corduroy trousers after the style of those you wear, and I'll be ready. Say, Thad, what a day this has turned out after all, and I was just thinking it the blackest ever."

"It's made me mighty happy, I know," asserted Thad, with tears in his honest blue eyes; "for I'd just hated to lose you, old boy, sure I would."

"Just to think of our launching on that great old river and starting for such a long voyage; it's immense, that's what. I've always wanted to see something of the old Mississippi and to think that the chance has come. Why, it's like magic, that's what. A flip of the hand and everything is changed. The opening of Uncle Ambrose's letter must have been the turning point in my life—our lives, Thad. Oh, I am so glad I hardly know what to do." "Ditto here. On my part I'll put the week in tinkering on the old barge, for she can stand some improvement, I guess. When that fisherman gave her to me on going to the hospital, from which the poor fellow never came back, he said he always intended dropping down the river to the gulf in her; but I never dreamed I'd be the one to navigate the Tramp that way. I can hardly wait to get back. I want to be at work making those changes, and building your bunk."

"Just like you, Thad, always ready to do something for another fellow," declared his chum, affectionately.

"Oh! shucks! that's where the best part of the fun comes in. And how lucky it is you've got a gun, Maurice, for there will be lots of chances while we travel down stream to pick up a mess of ducks, some snipe, and perhaps a big goose or two. Bob Fletcher told me he had shot 'em off the bars down the Mississippi."

"Right you are, Thad," cried the other.

"And if our supplies and money run out, why, we can sure stop in some place and get work, I reckon. Then there's fish to be had for the catching, and you know I'm up to all the wrinkles about that job, seeing that I've been supplying many families here with the finnies during the summer and fall. Say, can you come down tonight, and talk it all over aboard our palatial houseboat? We can arrange all the things we want to do, make out a list of supplies that are sure to be needed, no flimsies or luxuries allowed, and in the morning I'll get to work."

"Of course I'll come, after supper. Still in the old cove, are you?"

"Yes. I've got a stout lock on the door now, and every time I leave the shanty I drag my little canoe, as I call it, into the house. If I didn't some thief would run off with it sure. They're a tough crowd around here, the boys I mean. Wonder if we'll run up against many as bad when we journey along?" remarked Thad; and in good time he would learn that the Ohio and Mississippi rivers constitute what might easily be termed the "Rogues' Highway," since hundreds of tough characters make use of the current, in order to slip from one borough that has grown too hot for their comfort to another where they are not known.

But perhaps it is just as well that we do not see the difficulties that lie in our path, lest they daunt us by their multitude; coming one at a time we are enabled to wrestle with the trials and tribulations, and overcome them gradually.

Filled with enthusiasm the two lads plunged into the task they had laid out, and long ere the seven days had expired were ready for the voyage over unknown waters; the little shanty-boat had been thoroughly repaired, and changes in her interior made, looking to the comfort of the crew, and all supplies brought aboard that the limited means of the boys would allow; so that on the tenth of November all was in readiness for the launching.

St. George Rathborne

CHAPTER II

THE FIKST NIGHT AFLOAT

It was a frosty morning, but something more than that would be needed to dampen the enthusiasm and ardor of the two lads who pushed out from the river bank where a little creek flowed into the Ohio's flood, and started upon what was to be a momentous voyage.

Several of Maurice's boy friends were on hand to wish them the best of luck, and with the cheers of these fellows ringing in their ears they moved out upon the swift current of the river.

When the group of boys had vanished and the cruisers found themselves beyond the confines of the town they had called home for some years, all attention was given to what lay before them.

The boat had been urged out into the stream by a dexterous use of the sweep made for that purpose, and which, with the exception of a couple of long poles, was the only method aboard for steering the craft; and as it was not their design to get too far away from shore until they were better versed in the navigable qualities of the Tramp, the boys sat in comfortable positions and talked, watching the panorama as they drifted along.

Indeed, there always is something fascinating about such a method of travel that must appeal to almost any boy; for in spite of the uplifting tendencies of education, and the refining influences of homes, there remains in the hearts of most lads, and men as well, a peculiar longing for a spell of tramp existence—it is satisfied after a short period in the open and the wilds, when the comforts of home appeal just as strongly to the exile.

No doubt this yearning for getting close to the heart of Nature is an inherited trait, coming down to us from our remote ancestors, and will never be wholly eradicated from our systems.

And these two lads could enjoy it to the full, for neither of them had known the delights of a real home for many years—in fact Thad, never.

They made many plans while sitting there, and as time passed and new views were constantly opening before them, both seemed agreed that it had been an inspiration that had caused Thad to suggest this voyage, with the far-away Crescent City as their goal.

Thad had, indeed, done fairly creditable work in fixing up the interior of the house upon the float.

There were a couple of bunks that in the daytime could be raised so that they lay flat against the wall, and out of the way, since room was at a premium inside the shanty, with a cook stove, a table, a trunk and various other things filling space.

From numerous hooks in a couple of corners their clothes

hung; then about the little stove, which was to give them warmth and furnish the heat to cook their meals, several frying pans and tin kettles hung, while a tea kettle sung a soft song of contentment that seemed to fit in with the spirit possessing the two cruisers.

A supply of firewood occupied a box arranged for its accommodation, and there was considerable more of the same outside; while a new axe gave promise of any needed amount, dependent only upon willing muscles, and an ability to swing the same freely.

There was the gun Thad had mentioned, hanging from a couple of nails—true, it might not be called a beauty, for it was an old type Marlin, and much battered by service; but then Maurice had on many occasions proved its shooting qualities, and that, after all, is the true test of a firearm.

It was a double-barrel twelve bore, capable of knocking down even a big goose, provided the right charge was in the shell, and the eye that glanced along the tubes knew its business and could hold on the moving game.

At noon they were passing Henderson, Ky., and changing their course to the west, for the river makes a tremendous sweep before getting anywhere near Mt. Vernon, forming a gigantic horseshoe as it were, the last part of the turn bringing the voyager with his face into the northeast.

Throughout the whole livelong day the little shanty-boat continued to sweep along with the current, which was something like four miles an hour at this point though it exceeds that considerably when the river rises, or the wind comes out of the north and east.

About 4 o'clock they passed Mt. Vernon, for which both

boys were glad, as they did not enjoy the thought of tying up on this, their first night afloat, close to a strange town.

They were apt to be pestered by curious visitors, and perhaps boys bent on pranks that might cost the travelers dear, since some of these fellows would not think anything about setting fire to a boat, and laugh to watch the frantic efforts of the owners to extinguish the flames.

When the dusk was beginning to gather on the moving waters, Thad spied what seemed to be the mouth of a good-sized creek below.

As they were just then skirting the shore with the intention of pulling in at the first chance, it was not much of an effort to turn the boat so that they could pole into the mouth of the stream and go up it some distance.

Thad's steering oar seemed to work to a charm, and he was more than a little pleased with his work in that direction; for much of the pleasure of the long voyage was apt to depend upon the ability with which they could guide their clumsy craft when an emergency arose.

Fortunately the creek seemed quite deserted; they had feared lest some other boat like their own might have preempted their claim, and the owners endeavor to make it disagreeable for them.

Not that either of the boys felt timid, for they were both built along the line of fighters, and ready to hold their own with any chap of their size, or larger; but until they became used to this strange method of living they would rather not run into any trouble if it could be decently avoided.

Once the boat was secured to a tree ashore, they began to get

St. George Rathborne

busy with preparations for supper.

While floating down-stream Thad, who was a born fisher-man, and always looking for a chance to snatch a mess of the finny tribe out of the water, had kept a couple of baited lines dangling behind; and during the afternoon several bites had resulted in a couple of captures, both being of an edible variety, known along the Ohio as buffalo fish, the two weighing possibly four pounds.

Thus they were supplied with the substantial end of a meal without the cost of a penny.

Thad had cleaned the fish as fast as caught, so that all they had to do now was to slap them on the frying pan, after a bit of salt pork had been allowed to simmer, salt and pepper to taste, and then turn when necessary.

Meanwhile Maurice had made a pot of coffee, and set the table.

A cloth would have been the height of absurdity on such a trip as this. Maurice had settled that part of the business by tacking white oilcloth over their single table, and this answered the purpose admirably, besides being easily kept clean.

"Ain't it great, Captain?" asked Thad, as they sat there enjoying the meal by the light of the two lanterns hanging from hooks in the rafters of the cabin roof.

Thad had insisted that Maurice be the skipper of the expedition, because of his superior knowledge of boats in general, and also his possessing the chart of the rivers.

For himself he wanted to be called the Cook, and declared

that he felt proud of his ability to fling flapjacks and do various stunts in connection with getting up appetizing meals.

Nevertheless, it might be noticed that just as frequently the Captain insisted on taking his turn at the fire or washing the tin dishes after the meal; while the Cook was able and willing to stand his "trick at the wheel" when the occasion arose. This was, of course, stretching the imagination pretty far, since their only means of propulsion or steering rested in that sweep.

Maurice admitted that it was indeed delightful, and the look on his face quite satisfied the anxious Thad that as yet he could not see the slightest cloud on the horizon to make him regret starting.

For bread they had brought several loaves along; neither of them had the nerve to think of baking the staff of life in that disreputable oven, even had they known how.

Later on, however, Maurice did turn out some "pretty fair" biscuits—that is, the boys thought them good, and they were the ones to say, since it was their appetites that had to be satisfied, not those of some finicky girl who might have turned up her nose in horror at the "abominations" these lads called fine.

Thad smoked, while Maurice had never taken to the habit as yet; but he did not dislike the odor of tobacco, and hence his chum was not compelled to always enjoy the solace of his pipe outdoors in uncongenial weather, though as a rule he preferred to sit there by the rudder and puff away, while his thoughts ran riot, as those of a boy usually will.

When the meal was over and the dishes washed, marking the

St. George Rathborne

close of their first day, the lights were extinguished and the boys sat outside for a short time.

With the gathering of night, however, the air was growing colder again, so that they were soon glad to seek the shelter of the cabin.

Maurice made sure to draw the shades fully over the windows, for he did not wish to advertise the fact of their being in that cove to every passerby.

They knew that a road ran close to the water, having heard a wagon passing over a bridge not fifty feet away earlier in the evening.

One thing they had been wise in doing—while the little boat that trailed behind the larger craft could not be said to possess any particular pecuniary value, it was of considerable necessity to the travelers, and represented their only means of getting around in a hurry, or going ashore when the water was too shallow to admit of the flat reaching the bank.

In order to prevent possible loss from some prank of mischiefvous boys or thieving negroes, Maurice had secured a long and stout chain, with a padlock, and at night this was so attached to the dinky that no one could sneak the stumpy little craft away without the use of a hatchet to chop out the staple; and while this was being done the owners of the Tramp would surely be getting extremely busy also with gun and axe.

"How does it go?" asked the owner of the shanty-boat, as he saw Maurice settle down in his bunk, and draw the blankets around him with the air of one who did not expect to be disturbed for a long spell.

"Hunky-dory. Beats my old bed at home by a long shot. There's no use talking, Thad, you're built for a carpenter, sure pop, and if there's any vacancy aboard the CAMPERTOWN in that line I'm going to induce Uncle Ambrose to let you fill it. Douse the glim whenever you're ready, Cook. I hope I won't have to crawl out of this bully berth until morning," was the reply of the other, that brought a smile of satisfaction to Thad's face, for it is always pleasant to know that one's labor is appreciated.

So Thad blew out the one lantern which they had been using since coming in the second time, and then crawled into his own bunk. As he had been occupying this for half a year or more of course he was very familiar with its features, both good and poor and made no comment as he retired.

The two boys soon passed into the land of slumber, and as the hours drew on no sound arose to waken them; indeed, outside all was still save the gurgle of the great river near at hand, the swishing of running water against the sturdy bow of the shanty-boat, a hoarse cry from some bird that fluttered along the shore looking for food, possibly a night heron passing over, and once or twice the hoarse whistle of some steamboat breasting the current of the mighty Ohio.

And the first night of their eventful cruise passed away, with everything well when the peep of dawn aroused them from slumber to a new day.

St. George Rathborne

CHAPTER III

UNWELCOME VISITORS

"Hello, Maurice!"

The call came from Thad, who had been the first to step outdoors after getting into his clothes.

"What now?" came the muffled answer, for Maurice was pulling a sweater over his head at the moment.

"Come out here, will you. We're in a peck of trouble, I reckon," continued the voice from beyond the door; and accordingly Maurice made haste to leave the cabin.

He found Thad with a pole in his hand, shoving against the bank until he was as red as a turkey gobbler in the face.

"What's doing here—why all this scrimmage?" naturally sprang from the lips of the mystified one.

"Stuck fast—river taken a sudden notion to go down while we snoozed, and has left us on the mud. I don't seem able to budge the thing an inch; but perhaps the two of us might," returned Thad, grinning sheepishly as he contemplated the result of their indiscretion.

Maurice grasped the significance of the situation and looked grave.

The river, as he well knew, was always a freakish thing, and apt to rise or fall at any time, according to the amount of rainfall along its feeders.

Just now it had commenced to rapidly decline, and as a result the shanty-boat had been grounded.

As it was a heavy affair, once let it fairly settle upon the ooze of the creek bed and no power they could bring to bear would be sufficient to start it on its way; and hence they must stay there, marooned, until the river took a notion to rise again, which might be in a day, a week or three months.

That was a pleasant lookout for a couple of boys bound south, and with winter close upon their heels—in a week or two they might be frozen in so securely that there would be no possibility of release until spring.

No wonder, then, that Maurice looked serious as he sprang to the side of the boat and stared over at the water of the creek.

It was running out—they should have known of the danger upon hearing the gurgle during the night; but somehow, lacking experience, they had thought nothing of it save that the sound was a musical lullaby, soothing them to slumber.

They would know better another time, and not fasten their craft to the shore in a shallow creek when the river was at a stand or falling; it takes experience to learn some of the tricky ways of these western rivers; but once understood the cruiser is not apt to be caught a second time. Maurice snatched up the second pole and threw his weight upon it, while Thad also strained himself to the utmost; they could

St. George Rathborne

feel the boat move ever so little, but it was most discouraging, to be sure.

Some other means must be employed if they hoped to get the Tramp off the slimy bed before she settled there for good.

Maurice was equal to the occasion.

"The block and tackle does it!" he exclaimed, darting into the cabin.

What mattered it if the rope was second hand, and the block creaked for want of grease—that last fault was speedily rectified; and having fastened one end of the line to a tree on the opposite side of the creek, the boys secured a purchase and then exerted themselves to the utmost.

It was a success, for now they had a firm foundation, whereas with the poles it was partly a case of lost force, the soft nature of the ground preventing them from doing their best.

Impulsive Thad gave a cheer when the boat began to move in response to their united endeavor, and presently glided off her slippery bed into the deeper channel of the creek.

"A close shave," declared Maurice, wiping the perspiration from his forehead, and surveying the late resting place of the shanty-boat with satisfaction.

"I should remark," echoed his chum, dancing a hornpipe on the deck; "just think what if we had been stuck here a week or two; all our grub gone, and the dickens to pay with our plans. Never again for me. I'm going to be the most careful chap when it comes to lying up to a bank with this craft you ever saw."

"I'll get the line loose while you start up the fire. Then we'll push out of here and cook breakfast while we float downstream. Every mile made now may save us trouble later; for you know what old Pap Larkin told us about sudden freezes coming sometimes in November, and we want to get in the big river before we strike anything like that."

In less than ten minutes they were moving out of the mouth of the creek, with the river, half wreathed in fog, lying before them.

"We'll have to keep a good lookout, unless we want to run a chance of cutting down some river steamer coming upstream," laughed Thad.

"Oh, that's easily avoided by keeping close in by the shore until this mist rises, which I calculate it will do by 9 o'clock or so," replied Maurice, using his pole to advantage, so as to send the boat out upon the current of the river, where they were speedily moving merrily along.

It was a delight to cook breakfast with such surroundings, and a constantly changing panorama along the shore.

Never did bacon have such a delicious odor; and when the coffee boiled up, sending its fragrance throughout the cabin and out of the partly open door, Maurice, who was attending to the steering part of the business at the time, loudly bewailed the fact that he must wait five long minutes more ere satisfying the craving appetite that these suggestions of breakfast put on edge.

While they were still eating they passed a place on the Kentucky side that from the map they believed to be Uniontown, which proved that they were making fair progress while sitting around—which is one of the finest

St. George Rathborne

things in connection with drifting south.

As Maurice said it reminded him of a garden that grew while the proprietor slept, for they could count on so many miles a day with ordinary good luck, and not a hand put out to urge the craft along.

While both these boys had spent much of their lives upon the banks of the Ohio, and were accustomed to the various sights familiar to all river dwellers, at the same time things had a vastly different appearance now that they were afloat and actually drawing a little nearer and nearer to the sunny southland with each passing hour.

They were in good spirits all the time, and hailed other voyagers with the customary salutations suitable to the occasion.

It became no unusual thing to see one or two flatboats with cabins something like their own, either drifting lazily along the stream or tied up close to the bank; for, as has been said before, the river is a muchly traveled highway, and the types of people that make use of it in their annual pilgrimages south must prove of tremendous interest to any one fond of studying humanity.

It was a banner day for the travelers, clear and fairly pleasant, one that in the rougher times ahead would always be looked back to as a period to be envied.

They made great progress, too, and when the afternoon sun waning in the west warned them that it was time to keep their eyes about for a decent place in which to pass the night, Maurice calculated that they had come all of forty miles since morning, which was making quite a gap in the distance separating them from the junction of the two rivers.

The air was growing colder, and Thad, who professed to be something of a weather sharp, declared that they were in for a touch of winter very speedily, which made them both long to get out of the clutches of the Ohio before ice formed and impeded their progress.

Maurice scouted any chance of this happening; it might have been more serious had they been cruising in a small boat which must find a safe harbor every night in some creek; because it might grow cold enough to freeze such a craft in some night, or at least shut those harbors of refuge to entrance; but with such a big and stanch craft they could tie up to the shore and pay little attention to the in-rolling waves cast by the suction of passing steam-boats.

This night they found a chance to secure the shanty-boat to some rocks; and as the neighborhood seemed lonely, they chose to go ashore and build a fire on the sandy stretch that ran under the shelving bank.

Just for a change they cooked supper ashore, too, for it would be seldom that this sort of an opportunity might come to them, and they felt that they ought to take advantage of it while it lasted.

Already had the wind shifted to the northwest, and it was cold enough to make them seek the leeward side of the fire while eating supper.

They had gone aboard to see about the fire, and Maurice was lying on a bed of dead grass and moss looking into the glowing depths of the fire and allowing his thoughts to go out to the wonderful possibilities of the beckoning future, with Uncle Ambrose as the good fairy who was to lead him into strange lands that he had always wanted to see, when a bit of turf falling upon his arm caused him to suddenly glance upward.

To his surprise and a little to his consternation he beheld three black faces surveying him from over the edge of the bank; nor did he fancy the expression that could be seen upon the said countenances.

Upon seeing that their presence was no longer unknown to the boy below, the trio of darkies dropped over the bank.

Closer inspection failed to add to the good opinion of Maurice, for the fellows bore all the earmarks of desperadoes, possibly belonging to that class of nomads who prowl along the shores of these western rivers, picking up a living by doing odd jobs, and stealing whenever they think it can be done with safety.

"Hello, boss! Done takin' it easy, I spects. Got any 'jections ter weuns warmin' up a little by dat fiah? Gittin' powful cold, boss, an' it jes' happens we ain't got nary a match in our clo's, dat's a fack," said the leader, advancing eagerly and holding out his hands toward the blaze.

"Why, of course not, boys; make yourselves at home. I was just going aboard anyway, and the fire's yours," remarked Maurice, rising.

He saw the three roughs looks quickly toward each other, and noted that one of them had slipped between him and the boat, as though it might be their intention to prevent his leaving.

It was evident that there was trouble brewing, and unless it was nipped in the bud something of a fight would take place.

That they would stand no show whatever in the hands of

these rascals, alone as they were in this isolated place, Maurice knew full well, but he would not allow himself to show any sign of fear lest in this way he precipitate the trouble.

Perhaps these men had been watching them for some time, and knew there were only a couple of boys on the shanty-boat, so that it would be useless to call out as if several husky men constituted the crew.

Maurice did not wish to come within arms' length of the negro who had slipped between himself and the boat, lest the fellow seize upon him, so that he was in a quandary how to act in order to gain his haven of refuge.

The puzzle was solved in a way he had not anticipated, for just as the wicked-looking black tramp was putting out his hand to grasp him, as he pulled back, a voice broke upon the silence, the voice of his comrade Thad, saying:

"I'd be mighty careful how I laid a hand on that boy, you there!"

CHAPTER IV

A LITTLE RUN IN THE NIGHT

When Thad thus broke in upon the little drama being enacted upon the strip of beach under the overhanging bank of the river the three negroes, as well as Maurice, looked toward the deck of the boat.

By the light of the fire on the sand Thad was seen holding the old Marlin in his hands, and keeping the frowning muzzles of the two- barrel gun pointed in the direction of the black tramp who had seemed about to interfere with the passage of Maurice to the boat.

Evidently none of the fellows were armed, at least with shooting irons, for it was almost ludicrous to see the rapidity with which they threw up their arms and showed signs of surrender.

"Don't let dat little buster go off, mister. We ain't meanin' yuh no ha'm, 'deed we ain't now, We's jes' de most innercentest coons yuh eber seed, we is. All we asks is a chanct tuh wawm our fingers by dis ere blaze, an' I reckons yuh won't keer 'bout dat, massa," exclaimed the leader, in a whining tone.

Maurice took advantage of the opportunity to walk around the fellow who had interfered with his free passage, and gain the deck of the boat, when Thad immediately turned the gun over to him.

Evidently the boys were in for a bad time of it.

These wandering blacks might want to lie around the fire all night, and sleep would be impossible for both lads at the same time, since there must be a watch kept lest the rascals rob them during the hours of darkness.

Maurice knew that it was best to take the situation in hand right then and there in the start; he also was aware of the fact that these negroes only yielded to force, and that any attempt to gain their good will would be absolutely wasted; for Southern boys learn that early in life, and so it is they can manage the shiftless population that is employed to work on the plantations, while Northern men make the mistake of treating such negroes too well.

Accordingly Maurice took the bull by the horns.

"See here, you fellows, we don't object to your having all the fire you want, but we're not going to stand having you camp right there all night. Go down the shore or up a hundred yards or so, and take some of the fire with you. Then one of you come back here and get a big fish we have no use for. I reckon you know how to cook it without a pan. Anyhow, it's all we can let you have, for we're on short rations ourselves. Dye understand, boys?" he said.

Maurice could assume quite an air of authority when he chose; it seemed to be a portion of his birthright; and these lazy blacks are quick to recognize this vein in the voice of anyone with whom they come in contact.

"All right, boss. We don't wanter tuh disturb yuh, an' we'll go up de sho' er bit. Dat fish he taste mighty fine, I reckons, mister, an' we sho' be powful glad tug git 'im, dat's so. Hyah, yuh lazy good-for-nothin' brack niggah, pick up some ob dat fiah an' tote it up yander whah de p'int juts out. Dat look good enuff fur dis chile. An' boss, ef yuh gut dat ere fish handy I cud kerry hit wid me right now," remarked the strapping leader.

"Get it, Thad," said Maurice, in a low tone, not wishing to take his eye off the trio of desperadoes for a moment, not knowing what they might attempt, for if ever he had seen jailbirds loose it was just then.

So Thad stepped around the cabin and took down the big "buffalo" that was hanging by a cord so that the night air would keep it in decent condition; it had come in on one of his lines that afternoon, and they really had little use for such a quantity of fish; indeed, both boys were already a little tired of a diet of the products of the river, and yearned for different fare.

The darky ashore caught the finny prize, and his eyes glistened at its size; but Maurice knew full well that this act of benevolence on their part would not serve to protect them a particle from the thieving propensities of the nomads if a chance were given to purloin anything.

In ten minutes they could see a fire up on the point of land and hear the loud voices of the three blacks disputing over various things—evidently they were a noisy crowd, and the prospects for a quiet night did not loom up very brilliantly. Maurice listened and his brow clouded over.

"I don't like the prospect a little bit, Thad," he remarked, as a louder burst of profanity than usual marked a near fight above.

"We're in for a tough night, it seems," sighed his chum, dismally.

"Oh! as to that, I don't know. It all depends whether we have the nerve to cut the Gordian knot," observed Maurice, grimly.

His friend looked hastily at him, for the fire was still burning fitfully on the shore, though robbed of its best brands by the negroes.

"What dye think of doing—running those critters off—gee, it's a big proposition for a couple of boys, Maurice."

"The running's all right, but you get the cart before the horse. It's us who are to do the skipping, while they enjoy that fish a little later. All depends on whether we care to take the chances of floating down a mile or two further in the dark, and finding a place to tie up. If we don't it's a case of floating on all night, and running the risk of a collision."

"I say go. Why, we've got an anchor, you know, and the current ain't so very swift near shore but what it'd hold when we chose to drop her over. If we stay here one of us has to be on guard all night, and even then I believe those black jailbirds would be ugly enough to try and burn us up or something like that—steal our pumpkin-seed boat perhaps. Yes, I'm in favor of cutting loose," declared Thad, eagerly.

"All right; consider it settled. We'll just wait until we think they're busy with the fish and then one of us must go ashore while the other covers him with the gun, and undo the line from those rocks. After that it will be easy."

Half an hour passed away.

Then, as the sounds had died out above, they fancied the trio of unwelcome neighbors must be busily employed in eating, so Thad volunteered to drop ashore and get the rope loose from its anchorage.

Maurice was a little skeptical about the apparent freedom from surveillance, and stood on deck with the shotgun in his hands ready to spring to the assistance of his pard at the slightest sign of trouble.

But Thad met with no opposition when he climbed to where the loop of the rope was secured over the pinnacle of rock, and in a minute he had freed the line, tossing it down on the beach where it could be pulled aboard.

When his comrade was again alongside, Maurice breathed easier; this was their first adventure, and it was apt to make a deep impression on both lads.

A dozen pulls sufficed to bring the rope aboard and then the poles were taken in hand with the idea of shoving off from the shore.

They had been careful not to let the boat ground, remembering their experience of the previous night, so this part of the job was not difficult at all.

Just as they began to move with the current they heard a loud yell from the shore, and looking up saw one of their late visitors standing there, surveying the vanishing shanty-boat with manifest dismay and anger.

His shout was evidently understood by the others, for they could be heard tearing along down the shale heading for the scene.

But our boys had now pushed the boat far enough out into

the stream to avoid any possibility of being boarded, no matter how bold the desperadoes might be; and it gave them no concern that the trio howled and swore and threatened all manner of things for being deserted in this manner, just when they thought they had a good soft snap for a breakfast, and perhaps fat pickings.

Thanks to the friendly current, the boys were quickly beyond earshot of the loud-tongued and chagrined blacks on the shore.

"Ugh! that wasn't a pleasant experience, was it? Did you ever set eyes on three more villainous mugs in all your life? Those scoundrels are sure doomed to meet with a noose before they're many months older, for if they haven't done murder up to now they're going to before long. I'm glad we gave them the slip. It was well done all around. Now to float on for an hour or so, and then see if we have any luck finding an anchorage."

Maurice contented himself with these words, but Thad had to skip around on the deck in his usual exuberant style before he could settle down to taking his trick at the steering apparatus.

Thus the shanty-boat floated on through the darkness, and the minutes slipped along until the hour set had been exhausted; then, when they were thinking of coming to a halt, the lights of a town appeared close by, and it became necessary to navigate with caution lest they strike some obstruction in the shape of an anchored boat or a dock where steamboats landed.

It was decided to drop down a little distance below the place and tie up, for as some of their provision were already getting low, it would be necessary to go ashore and lay in more bread at least.

When a jutting point shut out the last of the town lights, they poled in closer to the shore, and began to cast about for some friendly tree to which the hawser could be attached.

"There's a shanty-boat tied up yonder," whispered Thad, suddenly, pointing to a place where the gleam of a light through a small window could be seen.

"Let her float down a bit farther. We don't want too close neighbors, especially when we know nothing about them. There, listen to that dog bark; the little rat sees us all right. That's where we made a mistake not to get a dog to go with us on the trip; they're good company, and fine for guarding the boat. First chance I get I mean to have one, no matter if it's a mongrel yellow cur."

A man stepped out of the cabin of the boat that was tied up and looked across the little stretch of water separating them.

"Hello!" he said, as if seeing them clearly. "Going to tie up below?"

Maurice rather liked the ring of his voice, and so he made answer.

"We want to—is there good holding ground or a convenient tree, do you know?" he asked.

"Yes, half a dozen of 'em. I saw the lot before dark; and the swing of the current pushes in toward the bank. Don't get too far in, as she's lowering right along," continued the friendly flatboatman.

Maurice thanked him, for it was a pleasure to run across a

chap so different from the usual type of selfish, envious and profligate drifters.

They quickly sighted the trees, and Thad, jumping ashore, soon had a line fast around one that would hold them safely until daylight.

The man on the other boat had glimpsed them sufficiently to have his interest aroused, for they could hear him throwing a pair of oars into a small boat, and sure enough he quickly came alongside.

"Anything I can do to help you, boys?" he asked with so much heartiness that Maurice warmed toward him immediately.

Of course there was really no need of assistance, since everything had been already accomplished; but Maurice asked the other to come aboard and join them in a friendly little chat.

The trip promised to be lonely enough, with suspicions directed toward nearly all those encountered, so that it was a real pleasure to run across a good fellow like this who felt some interest in them.

CHAPTER V

HARD PUT TO KEEP WARM

The big, broad-shouldered man proved to be a machinist and clock mender, who was in the habit of plying his trade along the river every winter; he had his family aboard the boat that served him as a workshop, and there were certain localities on his route where they looked for him regularly—he was, it seemed, a jack-of-all- trades, and could after a fashion even tune a piano if pushed.

Our two boys enjoyed an hour or two in his company very much, and learned considerable about matters connected with the lower river that might possibly prove valuable to them later on.

In return, of course, they told Bob Archiable all about their project, and he wished them a pleasant voyage to the Crescent City, with much luck when Uncle Ambrose came to port.

The itinerant machinist told them they had undoubtedly done a wise thing in quitting their harbor up the river after the advent of those three roughs. He believed he knew who the trio might be, and if he was right they were the ugliest set of desperadoes in that vicinity, who would not hesitate to attempt any sort of dark deed, provided the reward seemed sufficient to compensate for the risk involved.

It was a real pleasure to run across such a pleasant and manly fellow as Archiable, and the meeting, brought about in so queer a manner, would always remain in the memory of the two boys as one of the bright spots of their cruise down the river.

The night passed quietly.

One of the boys came out on deck now and again, as they happened to be awake; for the incident of the early evening seemed to have made them somewhat nervous; but nothing happened, and morning came along in due season, with a lowering sky and a feeling of snow in the air.

Maurice went back to the town for supplies after they had eaten breakfast, while Thad took the dinky and paddled up to where the other boat was tied to enjoy a little more talk with the jolly owner.

He met Bob's wife, a little woman who seemed to thoroughly enjoy the strange experience of being a pilgrim half the year.

There were also a couple of boys, one six and the other eight, sturdy little chaps, who looked like chips of the old block, and only eager for the time to come when they could put their shoulders to the wheel and help "dad."

Finally they got away and waved a farewell to this friendly couple, who had conceived a sudden and abiding interest in the future of the two young voyagers starting out in the big world to seek their fortunes.

"We're going to get it in the neck today, I reckon," remarked

Thad; and if his words were lacking in elegance, they certainly conveyed a proper notion of what he meant to his comrade, for the air was biting, and the waves dashed up against the starboard side of the shanty-boat in a way that was suggestive of storm and little progress.

So it must always be in making a trip down these inland waters, where one is at the mercy of a capricious current save when a favorite of fortune chances to own a motor boat that scorns the usual drifting process, and speeds along at a ten-mile-an-hour clip, regardless of baffling head winds.

One day excellent progress may be made, and then come several during which it seems as though every deterring influence in the calendar arises to keep the voyager from making his expected distance during the hours of daylight.

It is just as well in the start to decide that nothing that can arise will disturb one's temper, and that with equally good nature the bad will be accepted with the good.

By ten o'clock it was snowing furiously, and the tang of the bitter wind that swept across from the far distant Indiana shore seemed to penetrate to the very marrow, so that the boys were constantly exchanging places, one bobbing inside the cabin to get warm while the other held the steering apparatus.

The snow became so furious that soon they were unable to see even the Kentucky bank, and then Maurice began to think they had better haul up before losing their bearings; it would be a serious matter to find themselves adrift on the wide river without knowing whether they were in the middle of the stream or not.

"We'd better haul in closer to the shore, and come to a halt, I think, Thad. It may be all right to run along in the midst of this storm, but I don't like it a little bit. In fact, that cabin seems good enough for me today. How do you feel about it, old man?" he asked, rubbing his hands, which, even when covered with a pair of woolen gloves, felt the stinging cold.

"Couldn't please me better," answered his chum, picking up a pole and feeling to ascertain the depth of the water.

With that wind blowing them toward shore there was little difficulty in making a landing, and after skirting the edge for some distance they found a chance to get a purchase on a convenient tree, when the trick was done.

All the balance of the day they hugged the fire; nor were they any too warm at that, for the furious blast seemed to find cracks and crannies in the wall of the flimsy cabin through which to gain entrance.

At times it fairly howled around them, and Thad suggested the advisability of their tying down the cabin with a spare cable, for fear less some tremendous blast of wind tear it from its foundations and send it flying among the treetops ashore; but Maurice declared he did not believe it to be quite so bad as all that.

As the supply of fuel was growing low it became necessary for one of them at a time to go ashore and use the ax to a purpose, so that during the afternoon the pile was replenished bountifully in this manner.

Such a night as that was—the boys had never passed a more unpleasant one in all their previous experience.

It became very cold in the cabin, despite the half-way decent fire they kept going all night, and their blankets did not seem

St. George Rathborne

to be sufficient covering to induce warmth, for Maurice was shivering most of the time.

A flimsy boat like the one they were on can seem like an iceberg during a heavy wind that sweeps across a wide stretch of rough water, and comes straight out of the Alaska region; then, the waves that were kicked up by its passage across the river dashed against the side of the boat and flew in spray over the very top of the cabin, freezing upon the wall in great icicles, and adding to the general discomfort, for in the morning they had difficulty in breaking their way out of the door.

About four o'clock Maurice could not stand it any longer, and getting up, he pulled on his sweater and sat down to make the stove red hot, after which it became fairly comfortable in the cabin and Thad slept on.

Luckily the storm was of short duration, and with the morning the wind seemed to have gone down considerably, with promise of a further mitigation of the cold during the day.

Of course, neither of the boys enjoyed such an experience, but they were of a philosophical turn of mind and ready to accept things as they eame along, making the most of the good and enduring the evil when it could not be avoided.

Lucky the lad who has been blessed with a disposition after this kind, for life will have a bountiful supply of pleasures in store for him, out of which no temporary adversity may cheat him.

They started downstream again after breakfast, for the snow had ceased and it was easily possible to see their course.

The morning packet breasting the current hove in sight a

short time after they cut loose from their night's anchorage, and it was always a pleasure for them to wave to those aboard these boats—never did the pilot aloft in his little house wfeere he handled the wheel fail to respond to the waving of a handkerchief—it was the custom of the river, and one would be lacking in common politeness if he refused to answer such a friendly greeting.

By noon they were making great progress again, and Maurice began to have hopes of bringing up at Paducah by night; but there were so many twists and turns to the river he had not counted on that when the afternoon drew near its close and they saw a town at the mouth of a river coming in on the Kentucky side, he knew it must be Smithland lying at the junction of the Cumberland with the Ohio.

Once again they floated past a town, unwilling to put in for fear of trouble with some of the rough characters usually found along the river front in all of these places.

Fortunately, after experiencing some difficulty in crossing the mouth of the Cumberland, which was belching forth a volume of yellow water that carried the shanty-boat out some distance, despite their efforts, they finally managed to find a place to stay for the night.

It was in striking contrast to the previous experience, for there was no wind, and the cold had moderated wonderfully, so that it seemed as though rain might be the next thing on the program.

They were a bit too close to the town for quiet, as sounds frequently came to their ears from a number of flatboats anchored just below the mouth of the smaller river that emptied its volume of water into the Ohio; these people were evidently engaged in having a high old time, probably with plenty of liquor, for they kept the racket going more than half the night.

Fortunately, however, they knew nothing of the nearness of the shanty-boat that had gone past just at dusk, and while our boys kept the door locked and slept on their arms, so to speak, they were not disturbed at all.

They were glad to get away in the morning without meeting any of the rough element belonging to those anchored shanty-boats.

Paducah showed up during the morning, after which they had a long stretch before them straight away into the west as it seemed, at the end of which they could expect to find the big junction city of Cairo.

IIere they would make a sudden turn to the left and begin to glide down the waters of the wonderful Mississippi, heading really south at last.

But they could not hope to make it on this day, though a favorable run seemed to be the order of things; it actually did rain, as Thad predicted, and each of the boys, clad in oilskins, took turns at the rudder as the boat swung along downstream, not far away from the Kentucky shore.

Taking it in all they had experienced but little decent weather thus far; that would come, they hoped, when they managed to get further along in the direction of Dixie, where the warm breezes would thaw them out, and allow of lying on the deck taking a sun bath.

The shore was mighty uninviting along here and seemed low in most places and marshy.

Ducks were numerous and the gun was kept handy in case they had a chance to knock down a couple, for it would be an agreeable change in their fare to have game for supper.

The rain stopped about three, and Maurice, who had been looking ahead, declared that if he could only get ashore he believed it was possible to crawl through the brush and get a shot at a bunch of ducks in a cove ahead; so the boat was brought to a stop by means of the anchor, and jumping into the little dinky, gun in hand, he made for the shore.

Thad waited after he had disappeared, being anxious to see how the adventure panned out.

About ten minutes later he heard a shot, followed by a second, and then Maurice came hurrying along to the little boat into which he jumped and set out in hot chase of his game, which was floating away on the current.

Thad pulled in the anchor and floated downstream; he saw his chum drag several ducks aboard, and so of course Thad had to do the Highland fling as usual.

CHAPTER VI

IN THE GAME COUNTRY

It proved that Maurice had knocked down three of the feathered prizes, and as they were fat teal, it looked like a genuine treat in store for the river travelers on the shanty-boat.

Thad was at work plucking the fowl before they had gone fifty yards down the stream, and announcing that they would have them for dinner that very night—at least a couple, for he believed one apiece ought to satisfy the demand.

"When I heard you shoot I knew we were in for a treat, and with the second shot I said it must be two; but you went me one better, Pal Maurice. That little old gun is as good as ever, I do believe, and my conscience, how she does penetrate. These bones are knocked into flinters in places. How many were there in that flock?"

"Just three," returned Maurice, smiling.

"I thought so, and you bagged the whole lot. I reckon no fellow could have done better than that, at least so you could notice," quoth Thad, holding up the first victim of his labors so that the shooter could see how plump the bird was.

"Yum, yum," went on Thad, swinging it to and fro, and gloating over the tempting appearance of the game; "don't I just wish it was time to sound the gong for supper and these boys browned and ready to be devoured. But three mortal hours must crawl along before then. How can I ever stand it?" he groaned.

Maurice was accustomed to these ludicrous actions of his chum, and only laughed at the wry face he made; but, to tell the truth, he would not be sorry himself when the night had settled down over the river, and they were lying in some snug sheltered nook, sniffing the cooking meal.

The birds seemed to be young, and it was decided to try the oven upon them; so Thad went in, after he had them both ready.

Once when the other glanced through the partly open door he saw him trying to make some stuffing out of bread crumbs. Then the fire was attended to, so that there would be an abundance of heat, after which Thad appeared with the look of a victor on his face.

An hour later and the first scent of dinner began to ooze from the door; whereupon Thad darted in and began to baste the fowl with tender solicitude.

He came out making motions with his lips as though his mouth were fairly watering, and shaking his head in a suggestive way that made Maurice roar.

Meanwhile the boat had been steadily heading down the river, and the same dismal prospect confronted them along the shore—marshy land, with higher ground further back, an ideal place for ducks, great flocks of which could be seen at this hour flying from the river to some favorite sleeping

St. George Rathborne

place in the marsh.

"If this were a hunting expedition, which it is not, we would not need to go a bit further than this place. Just imagine the shooting a fellow could have in the swampy land beyond— with some decoys he could bang away for hours at fresh flocks passing back and forth all day trading. Well, I mean to pick up quite a few now and then, unless we get tired of duck as we did of fish," Maurice observed, while watching these bunches of feathered squawkers sailing swiftly past the boat and heading shoreward.

"Tired of duck—why, you could never get me to say that. I could eat it every meal and every day for a month," announced Thad, sniffing the air, which was now becoming very strongly impregnated with a delicious odor that announced the nearness to completion of the baking birds.

And when finally they found a place to anchor the shanty-boat—for trees there were none within reach of their longest cable—and the shades of evening began to gather around them, Thad went inside to see if dinner were ready for serving.

Well, that was a feast the boys enjoyed to the limit—the ducks were tender, delightfully browned, and possessed of a flavor our young and hungry cruisers had never seen equaled; the stuffing proved to be a success; the coffee was as tasty as usual, and, in fact, they fairly reveled in good things until nature called a halt, and the board was cleared.

The night proved very quiet, and as there was now a moon of fair size, the early part of it was not wholly dark and forbidding.

And such a variety of queer sounds as came to their ears

from the adjacent marshes, most of which must have been made by the aquatic birds that spent the night there; but there were also mysterious grunts and squawks that kept both boys guessing for the longest time, while they sat on deck, Thad smoking his pet pipe and Maurice just bundled up in a blanket, taking it easy.

"I rather think if a fellow hunted around in that place he'd find 'coons and 'possums galore, besides a fox or two prowling around in search of a fat duck, for you know, Thad, they're like you, and can eat one at every meal, day in and day out. A funny assortment of sounds to woo a chap to sleep, eh? If you wake up in the night please don't think you're in a menagerie and shout for me to jump in and pull you out. To speak of it makes me feel that I'm pretty sleepy and that a turn of a few hours in that cozy bunk of mine wouldn't go amiss. What say?"

It turned out that Thad was about as sleepy as his chum, so after looking to the anchor to see that it had good holding ground, for a sudden storm coming out of the east would be apt to sweep them down the big river, extremely dangerous at this point, they retired inside the cabin.

The night passed without any storm, breaking over their devoted heads, for which both boys were thankful when morning came, and they looked out to see the sun painting the heavens red with his advance couriers.

Maurice was washing his face in the only little tin basin they owned when he heard an exclamation from his friend— whenever anything out of the usual occurred Thad always began growling and talking to himself as though he had an audience which was waiting to be addressed.

"Well, it's gone sure enough, and that's all there is to it. Now, hang it, how could a fox have come aboard our boat with twenty feet of water separating us from the shore? That's a conundrum I give up," Thad was saying to himself.

"Hey what all this row about—who's been aboard during the night, and what do you miss, Mr. Cook? You remember we ate those two ducks last night; did you expect they would turn up again this morning to be devoured over again?" laughed the Captain, still dashing the cold water in his face, and finally snatching up the coarse huck towel to rub his skin dry.

"That's all right, but it's the other chap I'm after now—perhaps you'll be so obliging as to tell me where I can put my paws on him. I hung the duck from this nail—the cord was good and strong, and it couldn't have broken loose. You see it ain't there now. So the question is did the blamed bird come to life again and skedaddle off, or was one of your friends the foxes aboard while we snoozed, to make way with my fat duck? Anyhow, it's gone, dead sure, and that's no lie."

"I see it is. Certain, are you, that it hung there when we went to bed?"

"One of the last things I did was to slip around here and nip it to make sure it was as tender as those jolly birds we had for supper. There wasn't any wind to whip it around and twist the cord till it broke. Yet where is it now?" and he shook his head dolefully, looked at his friend as if confident Maurice could in some way explain the mystery.

Maurice went at things in a far different way from his chum; instead of calling it an unfathomable mystery he stepped forward and took hold of the piece of cord that still hung from the nail.

Thad saw him closely examine it.

"Could a fox swim aboard and climb on top of the cabin to reach over and down to where that duck was hanging, and cut the cord with his sharp teeth, and then sling the bird over his shoulder to swim back again to—" he began.

"Stop!" exclaimed Maurice. "You're on the wrong track. It wasn't a fox!"

"'Coon, 'possum, wildcat, whatever could it have been?"

"A two-legged thief," announced Maurice, quietly.

"Shucks! you don't say so? How'd he ever get here, and if he wanted to steal why didn't he run off with something more valuable than a poor little teal?"

"H'm, will you tell me what he could have taken, with everything nailed down, the cabin door locked and even the little dinky fastened with a chain and lock. This cord was cut with a knife and never twisted apart. Do you know that once in the night I awoke and thought I heard something knock against the side of the boat—that must have been his skiff when he came aboard, and I thought it was only a floating log. Well, our teal is gone; but think of the lot over in the marsh yonder. The fellow must have been mighty hungry, and with no way of shooting a dinner. Why, while you cook breakfast I'm going to see what I can do with taking toll of our neighbors who kept serenading us all night."

Which he did.

Once in the marsh with the little boat and his gun, Maurice found that it would be the easiest thing in the world to knock over a dozen ducks if he wanted them, and indeed he held his fire from the first because he believed he could get several victims with the one shot.

Four times he pulled the trigger inside of ten minutes, and when Thad looked out to see if he were in sight, so as to wave to him that breakfast was ready, the lone hunter was just in the act of throwing a couple of plump birds upon the deck.

"Two—wow, that's good!" cried Cookey, in his usual ornate style, darting out to pick the game up.

"Four!" exclaimed Maurice, suiting the action to the word, and landing a second brace beside the first.

As Thad stooped down to feel of these he received a shock, for a third couple struck him on the head.

"Six?" he ejaculated, almost afraid to believe his eyes.

"That's not all. I'm determined to keep you on a duck diet for a week, so there's another brace, and for good measure count these as ten!" announced the mighty Nimrod, climbing over the gunwhale himself, gun in hand.

It was a pretty assortment of game, six of them teal, three mallards and one of an unknown breed, which Maurice thought might be a broadbill, though he had an idea that class of divers kept near the salt water in its migration.

"I forgive that wretched thief; he's welcome to the lone duck he took. Why, it looks like you'd enjoy nothing better than to agree to supply food for all the families in Evansville at this rate; and I believe you could do it, too, down here, for every time you shot, a million or two ducks sprang up above that marsh, and their wings made a roar like thunder. Say, I like this country around here. Given a good old gun like this Marlin, plenty of ammunition, a fishing outfit, and some cooking things and matches—yes, and a little tobacco for a fellow's pipe, and I think I could exist here forever without needing a cent. I'm awful glad I came, ain't you, pal?"

"Don't I look like it, Cook? See anything like regret on my phiz? I'm just as happy as I look, and the end isn't yet, for we've got several months of this before us; of course, there'll be troubles and setbacks, but in spite of all we're sure to keep making steady progress into Dixieland, and long before Uncle Ambrose gets into port again we'll be waiting for him in New Orleans. It was just the finest thing in the world that his letter should have reached me on that black day; and then to think how you had this inspiration, too—why, I consider that we're two of the luckiest fellows on earth this morning," said Maurice, earnestly.

"Bully for you, old pal; my sentiments exactly; and now, come in to breakfast."

St. George Rathborne

CHAPTER VII

A WILD BLOW

"How does it look to you—think we can make the riffle today?" asked Thad, as they floated down the stream, very broad and swollen at this point, as the low shores allowed the water just that much more expanse—further up, the Ohio is confined by hills that prevent its spreading to any great extent, even in the spring freshets.

Maurice knew what he meant, for they had only the one thought in mind just now, and that was getting into the Mississippi.

He drew out his charts and studied them to make sure he was right, though from frequent use he knew the same by heart.

"I can see no reason why we shouldn't. As near as I can make out we're now something like twenty-three miles above Cairo, and at the rate we're sailing along we ought to pass there shortly after noon—say by two o'clock anyway. That will give us time to move down a few miles and have our first night on the greatest of American rivers," he remarked.

"I'm a little bit worried as to how we'll get on. You see I've heard so much about the tricks of the big river that I'm nervous," admitted Thad.

"Oh, rats! It can't be much worse than the old Ohio when she gets on a bender, and we've seen some pretty big ones in my time. We'll come out all right, never fear, old chap. Every day will have to look out for itself. What's the use of borrowing trouble? Not any for me. Now, what could be finer than this view, for instance?" sweeping his hand around to include land and water, with the sun dimpling the little waves.

"Nothing on earth; it's just grand, that's a fact, and I'm a fool for thinking anything can get the better of a couple of fellows like you and me when we've got our war clothes on. Hurrah for We, Us and Company, not forgetting the old Tramp. Say, she's behaving herself some, eh, pard," laughed Thad, his face all wreathed in genial smiles again.

"She's all right, and a credit to you. A little cool and inclined to be draughty on a windy night, but taken all in all a thing of beauty and a joy forever. Here's to her—may it be many a moon before she's broken up into hindling wood."

So they joked and chatted as the day wore along.

Nothing escaped their eagle eyes on the shore, and from time to time one would draw the attention of the other to some point of especial interest.

Now it might be the peculiar formation of a point of land, some trees, a swamp with hanging Spanish moss, which, however, was nothing to what they would see further south —or anon perhaps it was some negro cabin on an elevation, with the pickaninnies playing by the door, and the strapping woman of the household leaning against the post, always smoking her clay pipe.

St. George Rathborne

Maurice, with the hunter instinct, watched the flight of an osprey that was circling the river brink with an eye to dinner; and later on observed an eagle drop down into a fluttering flock of ducks, from which he evidently took his usual toll, as presently he flew heavily away, with some dark object dangling below.

About noon they had a little lunch, Thad making a pot of coffee, and otherwise the meal was called in local parlance a "snack," which would seem to mean a pickup affair that could be eaten standing if necessary.

They wished to get this duty out of the way, for by the signs it was believed that they must be approaching Cairo, and as the junction of the two rivers is a turbulent place, with considerable craft moving about, the boys considered it wise to have their full attention fixed upon their movements.

After all, it was a mere nothing—they simply turned a point and found themselves upon a much wider stretch of water— and this was the famous Mississippi!

Now they were really heading south, and no matter how much colder the weather grew, it could not freeze them in and stop their flight to the desired port.

Just as Maurice had figured, it was two in the afternoon when they could really and truly say they were afloat on the big river.

In about a couple of hours they began to cast their eyes along the shore seeking a favorable place to tie up for the coming night—the mere thought of being adrift upon that immense yellow flood after sunset was appalling to them, though possibly by degrees they might become so accustomed to the rolling tide that it would cease to have the same sensation of alarm for them.

It was almost dark before they discovered a convenient tree close enough to the water's edge to serve their purpose; for evidently the river during its periodical seasons of flood had torn nearly all growth on the lower banks away.

Thad climbed up to this friendly trunk and slipped the cable around its base.

The boys sat there on deck for some little time watching the last flickering red die out of the western heavens; and when the panorama had come to its logical conclusion, with a sigh they entered the cabin to prepare supper.

In this manner did they spend their first night upon the Father of Waters, and it was as peaceful as any they ever knew. The river sang merrily as its little wavelets washed up against the sides of the shanty-boat, the air was almost balmy in its touch, coming from the south where the cotton fields and wilderness of pines lay; and all together the boys felt that they had been exceedingly foolish to imagine that anything terrible could await them upon the bosom of this majestic stream.

Ah! wait until the same river is seen under different conditions, and perhaps the old dread may be revived with redoubled force; for the Mississippi in the throes of a westerly storm is a sight to appall the stoutest heart.

When morning came they were soon under way again, and reaching out for another stretch toward that genial clime that seemed beckoning them onward.

Now they could notice quite a difference in the stage of the current, for with the increased volume of water it seemed that they were being borne onward faster than at any other time in the past.

All the way down it was policy on their part to hug the eastern shore; indeed, to attempt to cross that billowing flood with such a frail craft would have seemed the height of foolishness, both boys thought, nor would they have any object in so doing.

The river makes many wonderful twists and turns, sometimes seeming to flow almost due north as it follows its intricate channel; for it is a law of nature that water always pursues the easiest route, and seeks its own level.

Maurice had during the morning commented on the balmy feeling in the air, whereupon the weather sharp, Thad, had warned him solemnly that there was a great change coming within twenty hours, perhaps much less, for all signs pointed to cold and windy weather.

So much faith did Maurice place in this prediction of his chum that he insisted upon tying up earlier than usual that afternoon so that they could lay in an abundance of firewood.

It is not often that a weather prophet has so much honor in his own family, and really Maurice never did a wiser thing in his life than when he thus provided for a bad spell to come on the strength of Thad's knowledge of floating clouds and such signs.

For the storm descended upon them that very night, and coming off the river, gave them something of a fright lest they be wrecked thus early in their voyage down the big water.

Given two miles of river over which to sweep with fury, and a forty-mile-an-hour gale can kick up a tremendous sea, besides penetrating every crack and cranny to be found in a flimsy cabin, chilling the very marrow of the sleepers.

It was about two in the morning when Maurice awoke to find the boat pitching violently and himself shivering with cold, for they had let the fire die out on retiring, such was the heat of the cabin.

"Hi there, show a leg, Thad. There's something doing, and I rather reckon your plagued old storm's arrived ahead of time. D'ye want to freeze to death, boy? Pile out and let's get a fire started. Then we'd better make sure our cable's going to hold, for if we broke loose in this howling sea it'd be good-by to our boat, perhaps to us, too." was the way he brought his chum out of the bunk, "all standing," rubbing his eyes as the candle which Maurice had lighted pictured the scene.

Hurriedly dressing while their teeth chattered, the boys started a blaze in the stove, and after a bit thawed out sufficiently to go outside, muffled in sweaters and coats, to see what all this racket meant.

They found a wild scene there, with the waves rushing down the river most furiously. Already the atmosphere had grown so frigid that ice was forming on the side of the cabin where this spud and foam dashed.

Looking out upon the raging waters the boys shivered at the sight, even with scanty light from the heavenly bodies that were part of the time obscured behind masses of black clouds.

It was frittering snow, and the prospect of a spell of bad weather looked very promising.

"Let me catch you making any more predictions of storms; won't there be trouble headed your way?" shouted Maurice, with mock severity; whereat the weather sharp laughed and began to feel of the rope that fastened them to the shore.

"If the wind should change there might be a chance of our being smashed against the shore here. If it was light I'd say it would pay us to get the anchor out yonder to kind of hold the boat off; but to look at that water I don't think our little dinky would hold out five minutes," continued Maurice, shaking his head.

It was finally concluded to retire to the warmth of the cabin and wait until the morning broke, when they could decide what should be done.

For some time they sat there, now dozing by the stove, and anon starting up as some unusually weird contortion on the part of the boat gave them the impression that the end had come, and they were about to be tossed into the raging flood.

Maurice was just sinking into some sort of condition resembling sleep when there was a sudden wilder rush of wind than at any time previously.

And as he started up, thrilled with a sensation of coming peril, he felt a new motion to the shanty-boat that portended trouble.

"The cable's broken, pard, and we're afloat!" he shouted, as the equally bewildered Thad struggled up alongside him.

CHAPTER VIII

THE TERRORS OF THE STORM

After that one feeling of horror both the boys recovered more or less of their ordinary ability to meet danger, and overcome it.

It was Maurice who sprang to the door, and threw it open.

As he pushed out upon the narrow deck of the float he could not but be appalled by the sight that met his wondering eyes.

Just as he had suspected so strongly, they had broken away from the anchorage. Doubtless the rope had been frayed by some sharp-edged stone, and when that unusual gust swooped down upon them it gave at the weakest part.

Out on the river little could be seen save a jumble of foamy waters, that seemed to be tumbling wildly over and over, driven by the furious blast from the north.

Maurice turned his eyes toward the other side, for it was in that quarter his deepest interest lay.

Back of the clouds there was a pretty good-sized moon still above the western horizon, so that this helped lighten what

St. George Rathborne

would otherwise have been inky darkness.

Hence, Maurice could make out the tops of the trees on the bank of the river, as they were outlined against the lighter heavens.

"We're just humming along!" he shouted, as he noticed how the tree-tops seemed to be constantly shifting, owing to the progress of the boat downstream.

"The worst of it is we seem to be drifting out all the while!" was what Thad called, as he, too, sized up the situation.

Both of them knew what this meant.

Once they were swept far out upon the bosom of that madly agitated flood, and the chances of the gallant old shanty-boat remaining right-side-up would be very scanty.

"We must fight against that with all our might!" yelled the other, as he pushed back to where the sweep was to be found. They set to work with every pound of force they could bring to the front. Again and again was the long oar dipped into the water, and made to press against the rush of the current.

"How is it?" gasped Maurice, after they had been employed in this manner for some five minutes, each sixty seconds filled with anxiety.

"I think we are about holding our own!" replied Thad.

"Is that all? Then how can we ever get her in nearer the shore?" demanded his chum, forlornly, as he continued to tug away.

"Have to trust to luck for that," came the immediate reply.

"Tell me how?" implored Maurice, who somehow failed to grasp the situation quite as accurately as the other.

"The shore lines change constantly, you know."

"Yes, that's so; but we might open up a big pocket at any time, as soon as strike a point sticking out," suggested Maurice.

"Sure. That's what I meant when I said we'd have to stick everlastingly at it, and trust to luck for the rest," replied his comrade.

Perhaps it was because Thad had been up against hard knocks more than his friends, but one thing was evident— when trouble of this kind came he seemed able to show a better and more hopeful spirit than Maurice.

Another short space of time passed.

"Say, this is working our passage all right!" came from Maurice.

"But so long as we hold our own we ain't got a thing to say. And I think we're doing that, don't you, Maurice?"

"I did a minute ago, but just now it strikes me the trees kind of look further away."

"That's a fact, they do; but mebbe it's only a little bay before we strike that point, you know," continued the other lad.

They dared not halt a single minute in their labor, for fear lest the boat be carried further out on the raging river.

"How are you—feel cold?" asked Thad, a little later.

"Not much—I'm as warm as toast, all but my hands, and they're freezing. But where's the land, Thad? Can you see anything of those bully old trees, partner?"

"Mighty little just now; but I'm hoping they ain't going to give us the shake just yet. That would be mighty mean, when we think so much of 'em!" said the second willing worker, as he tugged and strained with all his power.

It really looked more perilous than ever around the bobbing shanty-boat, which was now being tossed about on the water very much after the style of a cork.

And if the waves ran so high close to the shore what must they be far, far out yonder toward the middle of the mighty stream?

Neither of the tugging lads wanted to picture the scene; indeed, they had all they could manage in considering how the wabbly craft might be piloted so as to once more hug the friendly shore.

Presently a shout from Maurice, rather feeble it must be confessed, for he was short of breath just then, announced that he had made some sort of happy discovery.

"Land! land!" he exclaimed, hoarsely, just as a shipwrecked sailor on a floating raft might cry as an island hove in sight.

And Thad could easily see the tree-tops again, outlined against the gray heavens; yes, they were closer than for some time, and to his excited imagination seemed to be even looming up more and more positively.

"We're getting there, old chap; give her another good dig, and follow it up with yet another!" he managed to cry.

"Hurrah! that's the way to do it! Again, my hearty, and all together with a will! She moves in, Thad; we're going to make the ripple!"

"Wait!" said the more cautious Thad; "don't shout till you're out of the woods."

But nevertheless he too seemed to feel that more than half the battle was won, since they had passed over a wide bayou without any accident, and were now once again close to the land.

How eagerly their young eyes hung upon those shifting tree-tops, as they hurried by; never before had the dry land seemed quite so glorious as at that particular moment; and they felt that it would be a happy event if they could but plant their feet again on it.

Maurice knew something of the river, but Thad had studied the oddities of the Ohio for many a moon, while living upon its breast.

He knew, for instance, that when a bayou was struck the chances were there would be a point of land jutting out immediately below it, formed by the dirt swept out by the erratic current.

And this was just what he was hoping to find now.

Of course the swift tide would never allow them to land on the upper side of that cape; but if they could only take advantage of its inward sweep beyond, they might succeed in getting into comparatively still water, where the anchor would hold.

They fought "tooth and nail," as Thad said, to accomplish such a result.

"We're passing the point!" shouted Maurice, ending with a groan.

"Keep working! The current sets in just below, and we want to ride along with it," answered his chum.

Then Maurice saw a great light, and realized what his comrade had in mind.

"The trees are further away!" he could not help saying.

"Yes, but the water ain't near so sassy; don't you see how we are pushing the old tub in closer all the while? When I say the word you jump for the anchor, and let her slide!"

"Oh!"

Maurice was encouraged to work again with renewed vigor, for hope had once more found a lodgment in his soul.

Hardly had ten seconds passed before the voice of Thad rang out above the clamor of the wind, and the breaking of the waves against the stern of the laboring shanty-boat.

"Now! do it!"

And Maurice, dropping away from the sweep, made a hasty jump for the place where the anchor and its cable lay.

In his haste he must have made a misstep, for suddenly Thad saw him stumble and vanish over the side into the boiling waters of the Mississippi!

A feeling of horror shot through the heart of the boy as he thus witnessed the catastrophe that had overtaken his chum.

He forgot all necessity for remaining on guard at the sweep, in order to prevent the boat from being carried out; but abandoning his trust he sprang toward the spot where he had last seen Maurice.

Throwing himself down on his chest he endeavored to penetrate the almost inky darkness that rested upon the water at that particular place.

But not a thing could he see at first; it was as though those treacherous waters had swallowed up his friend forever!

And just then he became aware of the fact that there was a sudden change in the movement of the shanty-boat, which instead of continuing to whirl down-stream seemed to be brought to a stop, and was tugging violently at some object that persisted in restraining her onward progress!

THE ANCHOR!

Yes, in his plunge Maurice must have knocked this over the side, and the heavy object, swiftly reaching bottom in that shallow spot, had brought the wild cruise of the craft to an abrupt conclusion.

But Maurice—dear would the safety of the old boat have been purchased, had he been swept away, to be possibly drowned in the flood, encumbered as he was with all his clothes.

"Wow!"

Thad heard this sound, although he could see nothing; and a thrill shot through him at the consciousness that it must have been made by his chum.

"Where are you, Maurice?" he shrilled, eager to lend what assistance lay in his limited power.

"Holding on to the cable of the anchor, and swallowing a pint of yellow stuff every breath!" came back in broken sentences, as though the speaker might be ejecting some of the surplus fluid whenever the opportunity offered.

So Thad gripped the rope and tried to shorten the extent of its holding; but he found this a greater task than he had bargained for, and indeed, utterly impossible, with all that sweep of the river to buck against him.

"Wait! it's all right, and I'm coming!" he again heard the other say; and this time it seemed as though the voice must be much closer.

Then he caught his first glimpse of Maurice, amid all the foam in the rear of the boat, where the onrushing flood failed to start the anchored craft from her moorings.

In another minute he could reach out a helping hand, which being seized upon by the imperiled lad, Maurice was soon brought close enough, to admit of his climbing over the low gunwale.

"Gee! that was a close shave, though!" he gasped, as he sat up, the water pouring from him in rivulets.

Thad was pumping his hand like a machine, and almost crying in his hysterical delight.

"Oh! you gave me an awful scare, old fellow, you sure did! I thought you was a goner, and felt like jumping in, too, myself. It would be mighty tough to lose you, Maurice, mighty tough!" he kept saying as he squeezed the other's hand.

"Well, a miss is as good as a mile; and the only thing I'm thinking of just now is a way to get warm. My teeth are rattling together like the dickens. It was just comfortable in the water; but this air cuts through me like a knife!" said Maurice, getting up on his knees.

"You must go inside at once, and I'll have the fire booming in a jiffy. Never mind the boat; I reckon that rope will hold us here all right till morning. When you are warm I'm going to come out and see if I can put another anchor of some sort over. We've got a rope and that fine big stone, you know. Shoo, now, and get into the coop, you!"

In this fashion did Thad chase his chum indoors.

He busied himself with the fire, and it was not long before he had the interior of the cabin feeling comfortable.

And while the boat pitched and plunged, yet seemed to hold her own against the raging storm, Maurice changed his clothes, and was presently feeling none the worse for his involuntary bath.

Long before this the other had slipped out to fulfill his programme with regard to the second anchor.

CHAPTER IX

GOOD OLD MARLIN

When Thad came in later on he declared that the chances were now that the boat would hold her own during the balance of that stormy night.

"Always providing," he added, with due caution, "that it don't get any worse, and the wind shift to the northeast, which would be bad for us here."

So they started in again to try and keep watch-and-watch, one securing a little sleep while the other stood guard.

It was only a poor makeshift at best, for what Maurice called "cat-naps" were the best they could do at any time.

That night would not soon be forgotten by the boys, for it seemed to be about forty hours long.

And as time crept on at a snail pace the howling of the wintry gale continued unabated, with the roar of the wind through the tree-tops ashore, the dash of the waves on the point above, and the constant wabbling motion of the shanty-boat to remind them of their peril.

It may have been a couple of hours before the time for morning to come along that Thad, after a trip of investigation outside, returned with some news.

"Wind's shifted!" he announced, as he came staggering in again.

Maurice jumped up.

"Then we ought to get busy if we don't want to be dragged out of this comfortable pocket again!" he exclaimed.

"Hold on, old fellow; you don't catch on. The wind has taken a notion to back into the west, and is now whooping it up from across the old Mississip," said the other, sinking into a seat, and holding both shivering hands out to the cheery blaze.

"Oh! that's a different thing. I reckon then we're more in danger of going ashore, than being sent adrift again," admitted Maurice.

"I guess the anchors are good to hold, if only we don't get banged on a nasty rock. I've got a notion there are a lot around here, even if we can't see 'em. But the chances don't amount to much; and it's me for another little snooze."

With which Thad sought his bunk, and bundled in "all standing" in sea parlance, not even removing his boots, for he did not know but that he might have to turn out at any moment.

But the next thing he knew was when a most appetizing odor came stealing to his sense of smell, and he realized that his chum was cooking breakfast.

St. George Rathborne

"Hello, there, going to have a midnight meal?" queried Thad, drowsily, as he sat up, rubbing his eyes.

Whereupon the other stepped to the little window, raised the shade and allowed the awakened sleeper to see that dawn was at hand, gray and forbidding, but daylight all the same.

"Well, all I can say, pard, is, that I'm mighty glad to see her come along. That was the most ding-dong night I ever spent, for a fact. And I guess I dreamed about you going in swimming with all your duds on, too. That was what woke me up just now with a jump."

Thad crawled out, stretching and yawning.

"Oh! you'll feel better after you've had a little coffee, and some bacon. Nothing like a hot breakfast to tone a fellow up after a bad night like that," remarked the cook, cheerily, as he started to transfer the various things from the stove to their table, with its clean white oilcloth cover.

Thad went outside to take an observation.

He found the storm still busy, and the sight out on the river was quite discouraging to a boy who wanted to get along toward the blamy Southland as speedily as possible.

Still, they had indeed much to be thankful for, with that snug craft to serve as a refuge while the gale lasted, plenty to eat aboard, and a supply of wood within reach.

"I guess the little dinghy would live between here and the shore," he remarked, as he came in presently.

"What's in the wind now?" demanded Maurice, already pouring out the amber liquid into the brace of tin cups that served them just as well as the dainty aluminum ones sported by some canoeists they had once known in their Kentucky home town.

"Well, you see, our wood isn't apt to hold out all day; and besides, there's another night coming for us in this place. One of us must go ashore later on and do some chopping."

"That'll be me, then, to start with. I'd like to get a few of the kinks out of my arms. Here, squat down, and begin work with that mess. Plenty more where that came from, and no bill to settle."

In this manner did the early morning meal progress, for the boys, having survived the perils of the night, were feeling quite like themselves again.

True to his promise, about nine o'clock as near as they could judge, Maurice climbed down into the dinghy, taking with him their only ax.

Thad had even been careful enough to fasten this with a piece of rope-end to the single thwart in the dump boat.

"If you should have a turn-over the blooming thing don't know enough to swim, like you do; and to lose it just now would put us in a fine old pickle," he explained, when Maurice joked him about the solicitude he was showing.

"That's it," remarked the occupant of the dinghy, as he balanced himself carefully in sitting down; "it might be hard to buy another ax down along here, and one as good as this daisy. Now, when I say the word, give me a dandy push, will you?"

"All right," and Thad braced himself for the exertion.

"I suppose it will be harder coming out again, with a load of wood. I'm glad you thought of that bully old scheme of dragging some of it aboard with a rope," said Maurice, taking up the paddle.

"I'll pay out the painter as you go along," remarked the one who was to remain on board the larger craft.

"Push!"

Having been given a fine start he plied his blade, and rapidly the little boat drew near the adjacent shore.

No accident befell Maurice, and he was able to land safely; after which he drew his small craft well up on the beach, before climbing the abrupt bank just beyond, by means of protruding roots of trees.

Thad listened until he heard the steady blows of the ax; and then he went back to some work he had been doing at the time.

It might have been about half an hour later that he suddenly caught what seemed to be an angry bark from the shore; and as the sound appeared to come directly from that quarter where he remembered Maurice had been at work, he immediately became quite concerned.

The sound came again almost immediately, and seemed even more savage than before. Following it he caught the voice of his pard raised in anger.

"Get out, you rascal! Hi! there, what d'ye mean jumping at me like that! Keep off, or I'll give you a dig with the ax. D'ye hear, you big fool?"

Apparently Maurice was in some sort of trouble, and as near as the boy on the shanty-boat could understand he had been attacked by some roving animal that had taken a fancy to try and assault the strange woodchopper.

Thad jumped into the cabin and came out with the little Marlin in his hands; but then he realized how utterly impotent he was to give his beleaguered chum a helping hand just then.

The boiling water lay between him and that shore for a distance of perhaps thirty feet or more; nor was it possible for even his sanguine spirit to bridge it.

True, there was the dinghy on the little beach, and the cable attached to its stern ran all the way to the larger boat, so that it was possible for him to tug away, and eventually bring it alongside.

Should he try it?

The sounds had grown even more furious, as though Maurice and the unseen dog might be engaged in something resembling a regular circus.

Suppose he pulled the dinghy away from the shore, and just then his chum appeared, eager to throw himself into it, his disappointment would be terrible.

But all the same Thad could not stand there helpless and listen to that terrible racket going on.

Why, for all he knew, poor old Maurice might be in hard luck, with the teeth of a savage hound threatening his very life.

And so Thad made up his mind in a hurry, for he was not the one to hesitate when an emergency called for speedy action.

He had laid the Marlin down on the deck, and applied both hands to the task of getting the small boat across that intervening stretch of water as quickly as human means could accomplish the job.

If anything was needed to urge him on to unusual haste it might have easily been found in the continual confusion of shouts, laughter, barks, and general confusion existing ashore.

Swiftly the tender of the shanty-boat came spinning through the water, until in a short time it bumped against the side.

Thad waited only long enough to deposit his precious gun in the bottom, and then crawling over the side himself, he seized upon the paddle, and dipped deeply.

No doubt he made the shore in much less time than it took Maurice; for there was need that he should.

The noise continued, from which Thad drew new hope; at least his beloved chum could not have been seriously injured, for just then he could almost positively declare that he heard him laugh again.

So there was a comical side to the adventure, it would seem.

Thad was in such a hurry to reach the spot that he must needs make an unfortunate miscalculation when attempting to climb up the steep bank, or else a root upon which he depended proved false to his trust.

However that might be the boy fell back again, landing in a

heap at the base of the little bluff.

Taking warning from his mishap that speed is not always an indication of ultimate success, Thad became a little more careful; and as a consequence he soon had the satisfaction of finding himself on the top of the river bank.

Here Maurice had piled quite some wood, which doubtless he calculated fastening to the spare rope, so that it could be dragged aboard once he had joined his chum.

Smaller stuff he would stow away in the tender, and thus avoid getting the same wet.

But Thad was not bothering his head about the wood just then; he could still hear the barking, and the voice of his friend not far away, accompanied by various mysterious sounds that seemed to resemble the dropping of a heavy body on the ground.

So he gripped the gun and began to move forward, steeling his nerves for any sort of surprise possible.

In this fashion he presently reached what seemed to be a little glade, where at some time in the dim past the trees had gone down, either in a hurricane or before a settler's ax.

Then the show was before him!

His attention was immediately attracted to a moving object that continued to leap upward with wriggling movements, and then fall back again to the ground, to obtain new footing and try again.

And each attempt was being greeted by disdainful remarks from Maurice, who could be seen dangling his legs some seven feet or so up in a friendly tree.

Thad breathed freer.

He knew now that his chum had been wise enough to take refuge among the branches of this tree when he lost hold of the ax with which he had been defending himself.

And since he seemed so very merry now, it was evident that he had not been badly injured by the teeth of the brute.

Thad began to push his Marlin forward, as though he might mean business from the start.

He did not fancy the looks of the big dog, which was of a dingy yellow-color, and as large as a two-month-old calf.

Possibly he belonged to some farmer within a mile or so of the spot; or it might be that he was a stray beast, drawn back to the original state of his kind by the call of the wild.

Thad did not try to find out, and indeed, there was no possible way in which he could ascertain, since the dog could not talk.

Maurice had apparently become aware of his presence, for just then he called out.

"Take care, Thad, he's a holy terror of a brute. If you shoot be sure you get him, or he'll jump you like he did me. He's mad clear through. Hi! look out. he's scented you and he's coming!"

Thad needed no warning, for he had been watching the big buff dog every second of the time.

He dropped on one knee, and threw the Marlin up to his shoulder with a resolute air. Thad could hardly be said to be an expert shot, for his opportunities to go out hunting had never been very numerous; still, he possessed nerve, and could aim straight, which, after all, were qualities standing him in better stead just then than experience.

The beast was coming all right, there could be no doubt about that; and his appearance, with that hair bristling along above his shoulders, was anything but pacifying.

To the kneeling lad the rush of a lion in the African wilds could not have seemed more fierce.

He waited just three seconds, until Maurice, fearing that his chum might be almost paralyzed with fright, gave a shriek to startle him into action.

But Thad had done the wise thing after all; he wanted the dog to get close enough to warrant the bird-shot to possess all the deadly attributes of a bullet.

Of course there was more danger of his missing entirely; but Thad's mind was fully made up that he just could not and would not do any thing of the sort.

Then his finger pressed first one trigger, and almost simultaneously the other, of the double-barrel.

The deafening report was accompanied by what seemed to be a piercing yelp or two, after which there was silence.

Maurice had jumped down out of his tree as soon as the shots told that there was no further danger of his being hit by any stray leaden pellet; and seizing upon the handy ax he bounced across the glade toward the scene of hostilities.

"Thad!" he shouted eagerly, as he ran, waving the ax in the air, and ready to resume the battle, if so be it seemed necessary.

"All right here, old hoss!" came the cheery answer, that made the other experience immediate relief.

And then Maurice looked toward the spot where he had had his last glimpse of his late enemy.

Something was moving amid the snow that covered the ground.

"You got him, Thad; he's kicking his last!" yelled the excited Maurice, as he gazed with distended eyes at the feeble struggles that marked the passing of the powerful brute.

By the time the marksman had reached the spot the animal had given up the ghost; but even in death he presented a ferocious aspect that made Maurice shiver.

"Phew! that was an exciting little time," he said, wiping his forehead, as though somewhat overheated by his recent exertions.

"Where d'ye suppose he came from?" asked the other, as he bent over the victim of the steady-shooting gun, and shrugged his shoulders at sight of the bared white teeth, so wicked in appearance.

"I don't know. Looks to me like he might be a wild dog; but perhaps he belongs to some shanty-boat crowd below here. I wouldn't be too ready to tell about this until we're well away. It might breed trouble for us, you see," said Maurice, sagely.

"But he tackled you without cause, and any fellow is allowed to defend himself," expostulated the other.

"That's good logic, generally; but the owner of the dog never looks at things from the right side. He'd blame you for shooting, and say we ought to have chased the beast off with pea-shooters. Well, he kept me jumping right lively up to the time I lost my grip on this old ax. Then I got up in that blessed tree, though I'll never know just how I did the trick. H'm! that old gun of mine is some shooter, ain't she? My! how you knocked a hole in the critter. That was going some, for you. Thad, don't you forget it, son."

Now that he was ashore Thad assisted in getting the wood down to the edge of the water.

Here some of it was fastened to a spare rope which could be carried out to the floating boat, when the firewood might be hauled aboard.

Thad paddled out first, so as to draw the laden dinghy after him; then Maurice used the second rope to get it back ashore, loaded it with the results of his chopping, after which the other did his part.

In this fashion the entire amount of fuel was finally taken aboard.

"I think we have enough to last us for some time now," remarked Maurice, after he had in the end allowed Thad to draw him out just as the cargoes of wood had been taken aboard.

And as Thad once more pushed a couple of shells into the chambers of the little old Marlin he shook his head, observing:

"I'd hate to think what would have happened if I'd just missed that ugly customer when I pulled those triggers. For he was coming at me like a house afire, and with blood in his eyes. But, I didn't, all the same, and what's the use bothering over it? Is the storm going down any, d'ye think, Maurice?"

But Maurice could not say that it was in the least.

CHAPTER X

"NOT TODAY," SAID THAD

"I wonder how long this measly old storm is going to keep us here?" Maurice was saying, that afternoon, as he stood on the after-deck of the anchored shanty-boat, and looked at the wild scene out on the raging river.

They had seen not a sign of life thus far around them, since dawn. Even the few boats moving at this late season of the year on the Father of Waters seemed to have been bottled up in such harbors as could be found conveniently near at the time the storm broke loose.

"You called me a weather sharp because I said it was due; and now you want me to give a guess about the end—is that it, Maurice?" asked the other, smiling.

"Well, if you can hit it as good this time, and encourage a poor ship-wrecked mariner I'd be obliged."

"Say, it ain't as bad as that. We've got a lot to be thankful for, I reckon, with this bully old boat to hold us, and keep out the cold. For one you don't hear me kicking," returned Thad, earnestly.

St. George Rathborne

"Oh! come off; you know mighty well that I'm the last boy to run up the white flag. Everything's lovely, and the goose hangs high; anyhow, it will later on if I get a crack at one on a sandbar further down the river. But what do you think of the prospects for clearing?" went on Maurice, turning to his chum.

"Not good for anything today. P'raps the old storm will blow itself out tonight, and in the morning we may drop out of here.

"Oh! well, it's too late now to think of going on today, so after all it don't matter much We can pull some more wood on board before night, and laugh at the cold," remarked Maurice.

"Perhaps we'd better be doing it right away, then," observed Thad, with a glance at the west; "for dark comes sudden like at this time of year, you know."

"All right. Get the ax and I'll see to the gun, Thad."

"Thinking of more dogs, eh?"

"Well, no; to tell the truth I had the master of one dog in my mind right then," came the reply, as Maurice entered the cabin to take the Marlin off the hook on the wall.

Thad looked a bit thoughtful, but said nothing.

Perhaps they were not so very far away from some shanty-boat that had sought refuge in a friendly cove from the gale; and he knew the general habit of these floating people was to harbor at least one dog to each craft, sometimes half a dozen.

That gun might come in handy should they find themselves

confronted by an angry dog owner, demanding the reason why they had shot his canine property.

So they left their home craft, and paddled ashore in the little tender, one at a time.

The ax was soon at work, and the chips flying under the lusty strokes of both boys by turns.

Thad had been more or less impressed by what his chum said. While Maurice worked with the ax he managed to sit by the fire they had started, seemingly to keep warm, but in reality because the shotgun had been leaned against a neighboring tree.

And ordinarily Thad was far from being timid by nature; so that it must have been some sort of prophetic warning that bade him stick to the camp.

"Guess we've got about enough, eh, Thad?" demanded the other, as he threw the tool down, and breathing heavily, sat alongside his chum on the convenient log near the blaze.

"As much as we can get aboard, anyhow. With night only an hour off the quicker we begin to navigate the better for us. Here goes," and with that Thad started to carry the chopped wood down to where the small boat awaited its cargo.

They were busily engaged in doing this, and had really managed to get most of the fuel aboard, with Maurice pulling from the deck of the anchored craft, and his chum doing the work ashore, when Thad heard crunching footsteps above the spot where he crouched.

Looking up he saw a bearded face thrust out from the bank; and almost instinctively he knew that the prediction of his companion was about to come true.

Was this the owner of the dead brute that lay not more than eighty or one hundred feet away?

Thad felt a sudden cold chill. He was certainly not a coward by nature, and had proved this at various times in the past; still, there was an ugly scowl on that red-bearded face that surely stood for new trouble.

And Thad was glad that he had insisted upon keeping the gun ashore with him while he performed his end of the duty of transporting the wood to the shanty-boat.

He also remembered that it was close beside him, where he could lay a hand on it quickly if need be.

Then the man spoke, and his voice was just as disagreeable as his face seemed to be—a heavy rumble with more or less of threat under the surface.

"So, here ye be, hey? Wot business hed yer ter shoot up my dawg; tell me that, consarn ye?"

Perhaps he said something much stronger than the concluding words; but that does not matter.

Thad gave the signal to his chum to pull, for he had the last of the wood stocked in the dinghy. Then he turned his attention to the man who had addressed him.

If his face was white it was only natural; but his voice did not quiver in the least.

"I admit that I shot the dog. He was trying to kill my friend, who was busy cutting wood. I'd do it again, and so would any one. What business have you letting such a savage dog loose?"

Even while talking he edged a trifle toward the spot where the gun was standing against the bank. The man might take a notion to slide down, with the intention of attacking him, and Thad wanted to make sure of his line of defense, like a wise general always should.

"Hey! wot's thet ye say? I got a boat just a leettle way below hyer, an' my dorg's got a right ter run loose. Ye owns up ye shooted ther pore critter, does yer? I gotter a notion right now ter give yer sumpin ter pay back fur wot ye done!"

He actually threw himself over the edge of the little bluff, being angered by such talk on the part of a boy.

Maurice gave a shout from the boat.

"Look out, there, what you're doing, or I'll shoot you full of holes!" was what he whooped; but since the only weapon they possessed was at that moment ashore it can be understood that he was only seeking to fill the man with sudden consternation.

Perhaps it did work to some extent, for the big fellow rather hesitated as he cast an apprehensive glance out toward the shanty- boat.

Those few seconds were worth much to Thad.

He had started for the place where the gun stood, and which, unfortunately, happened to be close to where the man had landed. Indeed, had the fellow been aware of the fact in the beginning he might easily have cut Thad off from his coveted weapon.

86   St. George Rathborne

But knowing the absolute necessity for obtaining a grip on the Marlin, the boy plunged forward, regardless of the fact that in so doing he had to advance toward the enemy.

His aggressive movement rather puzzled the other, until he saw the gun leaning there against the bank. Then he gave a howl, and also projected his bulk forward, evidently with the expectation of reaching the firearm first.

But he was just three seconds too late.

Thad snatched the weapon up, and drawing back both hammers, held it in a threatening attitude.

"Keep back, there, or I'll do the same to you I did to your dog!" cried the excited but resolute boy.

The fellow saw something in the attitude of the lad to give him cause for prudence; and he immediately drew up, throwing out both hands in a sudden spasm of alarm.

"Hi! hold on thar, sonny, don't ye pull them triggers hard! It'd be jest murder, 'cause I ain't got nary weepon by me, I swar. I didn't go ter mean any thin' hard. Corse ye done right ter shoot the ornery dawg if he war atryin' ter eat yer pard up. Yuh see I didn't know ther hull facts in ther case, I didn't. Let up easy, now, bub; drap thet gun, won't yer?" he whined.

"Don't do it, Thad!" shouted Maurice, dancing about on the deck of the flat in his excitement; "don't you trust him an inch, I tell you! Make him vamoose the ranch—tell him to clear out, or you'll pepper his hide."

But Thad needed no such entreaty on the part of his chum to know only too well that not the slightest reliance could be placed on the honor of such a rough customer.

He continued to cover the man.

"If you take one step this way I'll let fly!" he said, impressively.

"But I ain't holdin' no grudge agin you-uns now 'bout thet dawg. Reckons it's better the critter's got his, 'cause the missus sez as how he acted like he wos agwine mad," expostulated the man; but there was a gleam in his eyes that Thad did not like, and he would not take chances.

"All right, if that's the case; but all the same you threatened me, and I'm not going to trust you close. Just back up along the beach, and if you make the first move to do anything I'm going to shoot. Now, twenty-three for yours, mister, skidoo! We don't want your company; not today," said Thad.

The man looked at him. He must have seen something in the determined manner of the lad to influence him in reaching a decision. That boy would keep his word; he was ready to shoot if crossed; and the way in which he had killed the brute of a dog proved his skill with the gun he was fondling now.

"Oh! all right, bub, I'll clear out, if yuh sez so; but if I ever get a chanct tuh even up this hyer score I'm gwine tuh do hit, sure's yer born!"

He moved away, muttering, and looking angrily toward the lad; but not once did the latter show signs of weakening.

When the big fellow had vanished from sight, Thad hastened to draw the dinghy, which Maurice had hastily emptied, back to the beach.

"Just sit in it and keep an eye toward the bank, Thad," sang out the chum on the boat, "and leave it to me to drag you out here. That chap means mischief, unless I'm mistaken."

Since his own thoughts coincided with those expressed by Maurice, Thad was satisfied to obey instructions. He squatted low in the small craft, handled the gun in a way that any one ashore could not help seeing, and kept watch along the line.

When he was almost there he saw the man break cover, almost directly opposite, and could even note the look of disappointment on his face as he discovered how the boy had eluded his clutches.

He shouted out something which neither of them wholly understood; but there could be no mistaking the ugly manner in which that fist was shaken toward them.

"Don't notice him, and he'll go away soon. It's getting dusk already, you know, and cold enough to freeze his red nose."

Maurice proved to be something of a prophet, for sure enough presently the man, finding that his derisive words met with no response, concluded that lingering in the vicinity did not pay.

"There, he's gone," announced Thad, finally.

"A good riddance of bad rubbish," echoed his chum.

"I hope we don't have visitors in the night," remarked Thad.

"Um; so that is what was on your mind. Well, now, I hardly think that fellow, or any of his crowd will have the nerve to come here and try to swim out to us; and you see they can't get aboard any other way, having no boat. Still—"

"You mean that we had better be on the safe side, and keep watch?" suggested Thad.

"I was just going to say something along that style. It wouldn't be a bad idea, you know."

"Well, I always did believe that it's better to keep from getting a cold, than to be able to cure one."

But evidently the man must have determined that, with a gun in their possession, the boys were not to be easily taken by surprise, for he did not show up during the entire night, much to the relief of both young shanty-boat cruisers.

Perhaps he had no companions to back him up in a desperate enterprise; or it may be that the comforts of his own cabin appealed too much to him on this stormy night.

Be the cause what it might, both lads were satisfied to have the night pass without any alarm; though several times when Thad was on guard some prowling raccoon or skunk on the shore gave him cause to fancy that the anticipated trouble was on the point of breaking loose.

Who the man was, and what manner of boat he possessed neither of them ever knew; for they caught no glimpse of any craft just below their stopping place when eventually the chance came to continue the voyage.

CHAPTER XI

NEARING THE SUNNY SOUTH

During the second night the storm began to die away, and when another dawn came the sun actually shone, though the country looked bleak and cold under the blanket of snow that had fallen.

Just as soon as it was advisable they broke away from their holding ground and once more started down the river, which was still pretty rough; but both boys were so sick and tired of that place they wanted to leave it for new scenes.

They were a little anxious lest in some way the rough owner of that miserable dog would bob up and give them trouble, and not until some miles had been navigated did they breathe freely.

And every mile they put behind them meant that they were so much closer to the genial sunny South, of which they had heard so much. After this frigid experience they were of the opinion that they could not reach that balmy region any too soon to suit them.

During the day the wind went down, and when afternoon was waning they sighted the town of Hickman, which was not a great distance from the Tennessee line—the mere mention of this fact caused Thad to give a cheer.

Now, they knew that it was not advisable to stop long at any river town, for fear of trouble with some of the rougher element that haunted the docks, but as some of their supplies had become low, and needed replenishing, they drew in, and Maurice went ashore to make a purchase, while Thad guarded the boat.

Contrary to their fears nothing happened to give them cause for alarm, and as for the fellows around the landing, Thad found them about on a par with the usual loungers, good-natured chaff predominating. Indeed, one of them even made him a present of a little yellow cur that had a pair of bright eyes and an affectionate muzzle, which tickled Thad immensely, he had longed so much for a pet.

They got away from Hickman at a quarter to four, with a clear sky and frosty atmosphere that promised good sailing weather on the morrow.

The yellow dog was immediately named Dixie, and took to his new title from the start, being a lively little chap, full of fun, and as frisky as they make them.

He promised to be great company for the boys, and something of a watchdog, too, when the occasion warranted it, for his sharp bark upon hearing any foreign sound was enough to arouse the heaviest sleeper.

Thad declared he would now be able to sleep with both eyes shut, for up to this time he had been compelled to keep one half open.

Just as Maurice feared they failed to find any place at which

St. George Rathborne

to tie up as darkness came on, and it looked as though they would finally have to depend on their anchor and a stout cable.

As they slowly floated along close to the shore Thad's sharp eyes finally detected an opening, which looked very much as though some stream entered the river at this point, and upon pushing in to investigate they found that it was indeed so.

And so they rested comfortably after all, though Maurice was a little fearful lest they be paid a visit by some of the rough characters floating around the levee at Hickman, and who would suppose the little shanty-boat could not have gone many miles down-stream before pulling up for the night.

Fortunately for their peace of mind this did not happen. Perhaps it was the cold night that deterred them, or it may have been that Thad had made friends with the Hickman fellows—no matter, they saw nothing of visitors, and in the morning got away in grand style, with Dixie barking a farewell to the creek that had served them so well as a harbor of refuge.

So they continued on their voyage, always making progress when it was at all possible; and with each day's setting sun drawing nearer the goal of their hopes, the great city on the lower Mississippi, where Maurice was to meet his uncle, and speak a good word for his chum.

It took them a full week to reach Memphis, for they had poor days as well as good ones, and there were various causes to delay them.

Maurice found a chance to use his gun again one evening when they had tied up in a convenient cove. It seemed that the ducks had a liking for that very spot and from tune to time a little flock would come spinning around the point with the intention of alighting there, where they would be protected from the strong wind that was blowing outside.

As soon as he discovered what was going on Maurice snatched up his gun and with a belt of shells dropped into the dinghy, paddling over to the point, where he landed, and hiding among some bushes awaited events.

They were not long in coming either, for in less than five minutes a venturesome band of half a dozen teal came swinging in. Too late they saw the boat tied up in the cove, and wheeled to depart, when there was a bang! bang! and several concluded to defer their departure.

Out came Maurice, and paddling around he picked up three birds, to the immense delight of Thad, who issued from the cabin at the sound of the reports, and of course executed one of his incomparable hornpipes on the deck at the prospect of another round of game for dinner.

But Maurice was not yet done; this was pretty fair for a start, but there should be more to follow; so he once again ensconced himself in the bushes and waited.

His patience was rewarded, for in less than another five minutes more birds began to head in, and he was kept busy banging away, with such success that after the battle was over eight lay upon the still water of the bayou, while several more had floated off down the stream.

Not wishing to let any get away after shooting them, the young sportsman put out in chase in his dinghy, and succeeded in finding two; meanwhile Thad, with one of the poles, succeeded in retrieving five of those in the lagoon.

Altogether it was a banner evening, and no wonder they felt joyful as they sat around the late supper; for Thad, with his mouth watering, so he said, for duck, insisted upon preparing a couple right away.

It is not often a fellow can make a fine meal from a duck that two hours previous has been plunging through the atmosphere from the north with a speed of possibly eighty miles an hour; but all manner of things may come to pass to those who voyage down the mighty Mississippi on a shanty-boat.

The night in this secluded cove was another pleasant experience which they must always look back to with delight; so it is a cruise of this sort is marked by its red and white stones, the one indicating trouble, the other joy unspeakable.

Maurice was not yet done with his business as a provider of viands for the table, and going ashore as the moonlight tempted him, gun in hand, he prowled around and presently had his suspicions confirmed, for he came upon a fat 'possum that yielded up the ghost at the summons of the Marlin gun.

Thad nearly had a fit when he saw what his chum was bringing aboard.

Once he had tasted the animal when with some darkies in the brush—they had gone 'coon hunting with a pack of dogs and unexpectedly running across a 'possum Thad was fortunate enough to get a few bites of the animal when done—it struck his fancy and he had never forgotten the sweet morsel.

"I bet you had that rascal in mind when you bought those sweet potatoes from the coon yesterday at Memphis," he declared, shaking his forefinger at the other.

Maurice pleaded innocent of the charge, and declared that

the only one in the party at all able to prophesy regarding the weather or anything else was Thad himself.

"All the same I imagine they'll just about fit the crime, and tomorrow we'll see how you can get up a real Southern dinner. Now that we are entering Dixieland we must pay more attention to the fads that these people cater to, and 'possum heads the list," remarked Maurice, holding the plump animal up so that they could admire his proportions.

The way the little yellow dog jumped and barked made them suspect that he knew something about hunting 'coons and 'possum and indeed there are few canines in the South that do not; so Maurice declared that if the chance ever came he meant to try Dixie in that capacity.

There was one good thing about this voyage, and that was the fact of the ever moving current of the river—so long as they kept in its swing they could count on being wafted closer and closer to their destination.

What they had to beware of were the many false channels that led nowhere; or else after winding in and out for ten miles brought the traveler out upon the main stream just a mile below where he entered.

Closely each night Maurice studied his chart and at the same time kept in mind the warning he had received that this map was likely to prove wrong in many cases, so quickly does the mighty current cut new channels along its course.

St. George Rathborne

CHAPTER XII

THE LOST TRAP

It was a quiet evening.

Outside, the moon was just creeping up over the trees, and shining from a cold looking sky.

Out upon the broad river the current swept past with its constant gurgle and swish, ever heading into the mysterious Southland, which our boys yearned to reach.

Maurice was doing some sort of writing at the table, by the light of the only lantern they possessed, and which did not afford any too generous a light.

Thad was rummaging about, looking everywhere for a steel trap he had once possessed, and which now seemed strangely missing.

"I wanted to try it ashore the worst kind tonight, because I've never stopped thinking of that fine 'possum we had; and from the signs where we picked up our wood I'm just dead sure a family of the ringtails hold out," he was saying, as he turned things over, and looked in the most inaccessible corners.

Thad was gifted with a streak of stubbornness; when he wanted anything badly he hated to give it up the worst kind.

Consequently, although he had apparently hunted that whole cabin over from one end to the other, he kept "nosing around," as his cruising mate observed, rooting here and there, and muttering his disgust.

"I've been told that there's such a thing as putting a thing away too carefully, and now I believe it," remarked Maurice, as he looked up for the tenth time to see the other bending far over, and actually pawing into a dark hole under the sheathing of the cabin side.

"But you remember seeing that trap after we started?" complained Thad.

"Sure I have; but since that early day you must have tucked it away in some place that's just disappeared. Joking aside, I wonder if it was that thing fell overboard the other day when you were romping about the deck with Dixie?" continued Maurice, as if a new idea had come to him.

Thad had a broad grin on his face as he turned around, still on his knees.

"What's this?" he remarked, holding some object up.

"Well, now," drawled the other, in his Kentucky way, "looks to me like it might be a trap; and since we only had one aboard it must be the missing muskrat gripper. Where'd you hit it?"

"In this blessed hole, and for the life of me I don't remember ever putting it in there. If I did it must have been while I was asleep and dreaming."

St. George Rathborne

"Sure you didn't expect to get a rat, and try and call it a bally 'possum? Hey! what are you after now? Expect to find the mate to it perhaps. Think traps grow from seed like corn?" Maurice exclaimed, as he saw the other once more thrust his arm into the hole.

"Why, I tell you this ain't the trap I had at all. Must have been one poor old The Badgeley owned. P'raps he kept his traps in here. Say, wouldn't it open your eyes some now if I pulled out a second one of the same? Now, what d 'ye think of that?"

"I declare if it isn't another of the same kind. They do grow then. Any more where that came from, Thad?" demanded the boy at the table, beginning to show a decided interest.

"Oh! I don't know. Would you say that was anything like the breed?" and he continued to drag out objects which he held up until Maurice had counted five.

"Here, you've gone and loaded that hole to have the laugh on me; now just own up!" he exclaimed, finally, throwing up his hands as if surrendering.

"Honest Injun, I never set eyes on a single one of the lot before now. You can see they're awfully rusty, too, and need oiling, because they've been lyin' in that cubbyhole lots of months. I've had the Tramp nearly a year now, and the old fisherman built it himself, he told me, meaning some day to float down the Mississippi. Just to think that we're doing it instead of him."

"Sure there's no more of 'em inside that bully old cache?" demanded Maurice, laughing as he surveyed the pile of rusty traps, which no doubt has once been used by the former owner of the boat to add to his scanty income by supplying him with numerous pelts of muskrats in the swamp not far from the town on the Ohio.

"I reckon I got the whole bunch; but no harm in making one more try," and as he spoke Thad pushed his arm again into the dark opening.

Maurice watched him as if amused.

"Another, eh?" he laughed, as he saw Thad draw back, with an exclamation of surprise and wonder.

"No trap this time; but something else poor old The must have shoved in there for safe-keeping."

When he held the object up Maurice saw that it seemed to be a little packet, wrapped in a dingy piece of oiled cloth.

"Well, I declare, that's mighty queer. Looks like the old fellow used that hole for keeping his valuables in. Bring it over to the light, Thad, and let's take a peep at it."

Thad was only too eager to do so, for somehow the fact of finding a treasure-trove aboard the Tramp excited him not a little.

So he knelt down beside the rough little table that served them in so many capacities, yet which could be turned up against the cabin wall in case more room was needed at any time.

"Here, take my knife and cut that cord," said Maurice, when his chum had been clumsily fingering the wrapping that bound the odd little packet for what to him seemed an unnecessarily long time.

"Guess I'll just have to," observed Thad, with a grin; "since my fingers all seem like thumbs. Here she goes, then," and he started to use the keen edge of the steel blade.

"Wonder what it is," remarked the other, his eyes glued curiously on the packet, which was not more than five or six inches in length.

"Feels just like a book," returned Thad, starting to unwrap the cloth that bound the object in its waterproof folds.

"A book, eh? Like as not some sort of diary. I've never heard you talk much about the old fellow; was he educated at all, and could he write d'ye think?" demanded his comrade, with awakening interest.

"Sure he could. Well, what did I tell yo? It's a book all right, and p'raps old The kept a record of the fish and muskies he caught winter and summer. He was a queer old duck, though he did seem to think a heap of me. Wow! look at that, would you!"

Thad's startled exclamation was not in the least surprising, considering what had happened.

As he idly opened the book there was disclosed a little collection of genuine government yellowback bills, not one of which was less than ten dollars in its denomination. No wonder both boys stared, their eyes seemingly "as big as saucers," as Thad afterwards described it.

Mechanically Thad began to count the money that had come into their possession so miraculously.

"Three hundred and thirty dollars! Did you ever hear of such luck in all your born days?" he said, his face lighting up with delight.

"But it isn't ours, you know, Thad. He gave you the boat, but how do we know he ever meant you to have this money? Can't you just remember something that would explain it all? Didn't he say just a little to you at some time about it?"

Maurice looked anxiously from the pile of bills to Thad's sober face, as though urging him to exert himself to the limit to bring back to his mind some clue that would unravel the mystery.

And Thad suddenly became anxious himself; he cast a quick look toward the little window of the shanty-boat cabin, just as if oppressed with a fear that hostile eyes might even then fee fastened upon them.

So quickly does the possession of riches bring new troubles; up to that moment such a thing as a possible intruder had been far from occurring to Thad; but circumstances alter cases, and now they had something worth stealing—and he grew afraid.

So his first act was to push the money out of sight under an old magazine that Maurice had been reading, one they had secured from Bob Archiable, the itinerant clock mender, when aboard his floating home.

"I remember now that when I went to see poor old The at the hospital, when they sent for me, he told me that he wanted me to have the Tramp for my own. Then he started to say something more, but began to choke so he could hardly breathe. The nurse tried to ease him, but he died right there before me. I've never forgot how mournful like he looked at me. I always thought the old man was trying to tell me something more. And now I believe it was this!"

"That's right, old fellow. But let's look into the book. I see it has lots of writing in it, and perhaps we'll get a clue that way."

The book proved to be a rude sort of a diary, in which the river fisherman kept an account of the various little matters which concerned his rather monotonous life.

Now and then, however, there were references to his expectation of realizing some long anticipated pleasure; and the name of "Bunny" began to appear frequently.

"What do you make of it?" asked Thad, after they had read for half an hour; he relied upon the sagacity of his companion to solve what was proving a puzzle to him.

"Why, it seems to me that Bunny must have been some one dear to the old man. I kind of think it was a daughter who married and went down the river some time or other; for his thoughts seem to have always been bent on that coming trip away down in Dixie, when he grew too old to fish alone. But go on and read some more. I reckon we'll catch on sure before the end."

Maurice settled himself more comfortably to listen.

"Sounds good to me, what you say; and that's about my mind, too," observed the one who had discovered the treasure-trove, as he once more turned to the soiled diary to continue reading what the former owner of the shanty-boat had written, in his crabbed hand.

"Here it is, at last; just listen," he exclaimed, fully ten minutes afterward, and then he went on:

"I met a man today that had just come up from down-river

way. And he knows George Stormway well. He told me Bunny was getting on right well, and had three children. Last time I heard there wa'nt but two mouths to feed. But he said George was laid up sometimes with the shakes, and money mighty scarce in their cabin. Time about for Old The to make up his mind to just drop in on Bunny, and surprise her. If I live to fall that's what I'm going to do, sure. I reckon if I left here in October I'd bring up at Morehead sometime about the end of November. But It'll be a long wait till then. As I get older I seem to want to see the gal and her kids more'n more,"

Maurice looked at Thad, and perhaps there was a suspicious moisture in his eyes as he winked violently several times.

"The poor old chap never hung out, Thad. If he had he would be on board this boat right now, carrying his little treasure down to his Bunny, to give her a surprise. That was a tough deal all right," he said, reaching out his hand for the charts they had secured of the lower Mississippi.

"What's up?" asked the other and his voice was rather husky, so that he had to cough several times to clear it.

"Why, d'ye know, I was wondering where that place might be. I don't remember having noticed it; and p'raps it is too small to be put on the map."

Thad went on reading in the diary, while his chum placed a forefinger on the chart, and ran it slowly down. "Here's where we are, right now," he was saying, half to himself; "and down below—well, I declare, if that ain't the queerest thing. What d'ye think, Thad, we must be only a day's run, above Morehead. It's on the map all right, even if it is only a wood station, where the river steamers stop to load up!"

Thad had to examine the location to make sure, and all the while he was saying eagerly:

"It's just like all this happened on purpose, Maurice—my wanting that trap so bad, and not finding it, and then looking in the hole in the side of the cabin, to strike this! I reckon old The's spirit must have been pushing me along; and Maurice, there ain't but one thing for us to do now."

"Yes," said the other, nodding his head with determination; "this money don't belong to us. Bunny needs it, and Bunny's going to get it, if we can find her out!"

"Shake on that, Pard Maurice. I knew you'd say it!" cried Thad.

And then and there they ratified the bargain with a grip that stood for everything that was loyal and true.

CHAPTER XIII

THE FACE AT THE WINDOW

"What else did you find in what he wrote?" asked Maurice, after they had dropped each other's hand again.

"Nothing much. He keeps mentioning Bunny often, showing that she was getting more'n more on his mind. And twice he speaks about me, and how much he had come to think of me. I'm glad to read that. Here he even wonders if I'd like to go down river with him in the Fall. Ain't it a queer world, after all, Maurice? Just to think how things come around; for here we are right near the place poor old The wanted to visit, and carrying his little pile to Bunny?"

"Nothing else worth telling?" asked the other.

"He speaks here about feeling bad, and hopes it ain't his old trouble springing back on him again. Then the writing stops. I reckon he was taken sick about that time. I tried to nurse him, you know; but when he went out of his head I got scared, and ran for a doctor. Then they took him away to that fine hospital at Evansville, because he used to live there. After that it ended right soon."

"Well, I guess the best thing for us to do would be to hide the book and the money where you found it. All these months it's stayed in that black hole safe, and it can stand another day or so."

So, taking the advice of Maurice, Thad had placed the bills once more between the pages of the diary, which he carefully pushed into its former hiding place.

"Perhaps Bunny'll be glad to have his book, too. If she's his girl she'd like to read what he said about her," suggested Maurice.

"That's so," replied the other, getting up from his knees.

Maurice saw him look up instinctively toward the little window; and then spring hastily to his feet.

At the same moment he thought he heard some sound outside, as if a floating object had struck against the anchored shanty-boat.

It might be a log, as frequently happened, for there were many such drifting on the surface of the big river, washed from the banks above by some local flood.

Thad, without wasting any time in thought, sprang to the door. This had a faculty of catching sometimes, and requiring more or less labor before it could be thrown open; and of course it had to play Thad such a trick just then, when he seemed so desirous of making haste.

Maurice, seeming to scent trouble of some sort from the strange actions of his chum, waited to snatch up the old faithful Marlin twelve-bore. It had seen them through other scrapes, and might come in handy again.

Finally, after considerable exertion, Thad managed to open the stubborn door, after which he rushed out on deck, followed by his mate and the barking Dixie.

"What'd you think you saw?" demanded Maurice, as he discovered by the light of the moon that the deck was devoid of anything in the way of peril.

"A face at the window! Some man was aboard I Oh! I wonder if he saw me put that book away?" exclaimed the excited Thad.

"But where is he now?" and the speaker glanced toward the shore, which was a good twenty feet away, the gap being far too wide to allow of any man jumping it.

"There's something moving away below there in the shadow of the trees on the water!" exclaimed Thad.

"A log, p'raps," remarked the other, carelessly.

"But I did see a face, I'm sure of it; and if it was a man he just jumped into his skiff and put off before I could get out. I wish I knew for sure."

Thad made a move toward the little dinghy which lay upon the deck, fastened with a chain and padlock, so that it could not be stolen by any light-fingered coon.

"Hold on there, none of that. Let me catch you chasing down-river after an unknown man in a skiff. Why, he'd just as like as not upset you if you accused him of boarding our boat. Settle down and try to forget it all. I reckon it was only imagination after all."

But Thad continued to shake his head, and declare that he

did not believe his eyes could play him such a trick.

"If it was a man, Maurice, and he once saw all that money, why he'd come back again to try and steal it," he said, solemnly.

"Oh, I guess not," laughed his chum, holding up the gun in a suggestive way; "at least not as long as we could defend our property with this bully old shooter. But better make up your mind it was a log, and let it go at that."

"Wish I could," grumbled Thad, shaking that stubborn head: of his.

"Well, how about that trapping expedition—plenty of steel in sight, and a nice fat young ringtail would be just the boss dish tomorrow. Anything doing?"

So Thad once more consented to drop the engrossing subject of old The Badgeley's treasure-trove, and pay attention to the matter of supplying their scanty larder with meat.

"Nothing to hinder my setting the whole outfit on the bank yonder, is there?" he demanded, entering the lighted cabin again, and thinking how snug it seemed after a short time on the cold deck.

"I don't reckon there is, Chum Thad. If one 'possum is good, two ought to some better, and as for three, oh! my!" and he smacked his lips as if in joy over the prospect of a feast.

Accordingly Thad carried out his plan. With some dripping from fried bacon he greased each trap until the jaws worked readily. Then he went ashore in the little tender, bearing the lantern in order to make sure of his work.

Maurice sat there and watched the shore.

There was no reason why he should fondle his gun all the while, but he persisted in doing so; which might be taken as an indication that the words of his companion had made a deeper impression on the scoffer than he would admit.

In half an hour Thad came aboard again, with cold fingers, but a satisfied air.

"It's only a question of how many," he observed, as he once more fastened the dinghy with the chain and lock.

"All right then. I'm going to make up my mouth for fat pig tomorrow, and look out for squalls if you disappoint me," and Maurice, as he spoke, led the way inside.

Thad was very particular how he saw to the fastenings of the door, an operation his chum watched with many a chuckle.

"Say, if he has as poor luck opening doors as some people I know, he never would get in here without arousing the dead; get that, Thad?"

"Well, you never can tell about doors. Just when you want them to open smart like, they won't budge. Then, when you'd like the pesky old thing to hang fire she slides open just like the track was greased with mutton tallow. I'm one of the kind that likes to make sure!"

"Oh! I reckon you are right. Anyhow, we used to write in school that it's no use locking the stable door after the horse is stolen. But looky here, do you know it's turning-in time— ten o'clock as near as I can tell. Me for the bunk, right quick!"

Thad sat there for some little time after his chum had crawled into his comfortable, if cramped nest.

Finally he, too, began to get ready to retire. On these cold nights the boys only partly undressed. They did not have any too many blankets or comfortables, and it did get mighty dreary in the cabin after the fire went out, with the wind sweeping over that wide stretch of flowing water that came out of the wintry North.

But before Thad put out the lantern, he placed it just where he could lay his hand on it at a second's notice and also made sure to have matches handy.

Nor was that all. He quietly picked up the old Marlin, and deposited it alongside his bunk.

Then came darkness, as he blew out the light. Thad heard a sound not unlike a chuckle from the opposite bunk; but although he imagined his comrade was laughing at all his preparations for trouble, the fact did not give him much concern.

When his mind was made up nothing could turn Thad aside.

No doubt he woke up at regular intervals during that night, and rising to his elbow listened eagerly to the various sounds coming from without.

The little window was well within the range of his vision, and as the moon shone brilliantly without he could see its entire dimensions plainly.

But long ago an iron bar had been fastened across the exact center of the opening, since the former owner of the shanty-boat did not enjoy the thought that roving boys might enter and pillage while he was on his route, peddling the buffalo fish he caught.

It would have to be a pretty small individual who could force his way through that window; and yet Thad's fears induced him to observe it with considerable apprehension.

But the night passed without any alarm.

If strangers landed on the deck of the shanty-boat while the young owners slept, they failed to make their presence known.

Morning came at last.

Both boys were early astir, as was their custom; the coming of daylight served to lure them from their bunks; and indeed on many occasions they would have been getting breakfast before, only that there was need of husbanding their scanty stock of oil.

Maurice, knowing that his chum was eager to learn whether any spoils had fallen to his traps, volunteered to cook the limited morning meal, while Thad paddled ashore.

He was almost through, and the coffee was giving a most appetizing odor to the surrounding air, when the trapper came paddling out.

Maurice watched operations with more or less interest.

First of all Thad threw the traps aboard, trying to look disappointed while so doing.

"Oh! come off, you!" cried his chum, who could see that there was something assumed in the actions of the returned sportsman; "think I don't just glimpse a tail like a round file sticking up over the gunnel? Just as you said last night, it's only a question of HOW MANY."

"One!" said Thad, as he tossed a young 'possum on deck.

"But that tail is still there!" cried his comrade.

"Two!"

"My! you make my mouth water some. That tail—"

"Three, and that takes your old tail. Now, what d'ye say to that for good hick. Ain't we going to live high for a while? I don't suppose you happened to see anything suspicious around?" and Thad, as he spoke, handed up the gun which he had made sure to carry with him "in case any more vicious dogs chanced to be roaming near by," he had explained at the time he departed.

"Why, no, of course not; but what makes you ask such a silly question as that, Thad?"

"Silly it may be, but I give you my word I heard a man cough just as I climbed into the dinghy," asserted Thad.

But Maurice only smiled. Truth to tell he felt positive that there had been nothing to the scare of the preceding night. Surely the ordinarily alert Dixie must have barked had any stranger been moving about on the deck while they sat in the cabin.

They were soon busy at the table. On the preceding day they had been fortunate enough to buy a loaf of bread from a woman on a canal-boat that was tied to the bank, her husband being temporarily employed at some work on shore.

Butter they had none, but the sharp appetites for which the outdoor life was responsible, craved none, and things tasted good at all times; the only anxiety that arose was in connection of quantity.

"Wood's mighty low, and as there's a chance of bad weather today, after that red in the sky this morning, I move we lay in a stock while we have the chance."

"Second the motion," quickly added Thad.

"All right. I'll rig up our endless carry then, while you clear the table, after you get enough to eat," and Maurice went out on the deck, where he could be heard working with the little tender.

Thad looked after him, and scratched his head. Then he did a most extraordinary thing, which was nothing more or less than reaching down and taking the packet from the hole in the wall, stripping the cover from the book, and wrapping up a piece of wood in its place.

Then he thrust the deception in the hole, and after a look about him hid the diary, with its precious contents, INSIDE THE COFFEEPOT, which he had emptied of its contents, and cleaned.

Perhaps he was playing a practical joke on his chum; but his face was too sober to indicate this.

The probability was that Thad felt uneasy, and as both of them were apt to be away from the craft at the same time, in the process of wood gathering, he intended to make things as secure as possible during his absence.

Which was conclusive evidence that at least he had not

changed his mind concerning the fact of a human face having been pressed against that little window on the previous night.

CHAPTER XIV

"MOREHEAD—OR BUST!"

When Thad came out he found that his comrade had gone ashore, taking the ax with him.

Indeed, the sound of lusty blows told that he was already hard at work, securing a supply of the necessary fuel.

Thad shut the door of the cabin.

He would have locked it, no doubt, only that it happened Maurice had the key in his pocket just then.

So Thad shrugged his shoulders, and dragging the little ferry-boat over the twenty feet of water he pulled himself ashore.

It was easy to locate the chopper by the sounds that arose; and so he soon joined his mate, ready to spell him in the labor entailed by the necessity for fuel.

The wood burned so quickly, with a strong draught always causing the stove to roar, that large quantities of fuel were absolutely necessary.

St. George Rathborne

Both boys handled an ax first-rate, and indeed, Thad could equal many an experienced woodsman in the accuracy of his strokes; while Maurice was not far behind him.

When the chance came, and Maurice stopped for a breathing spell, the second relay came into action; and once more the chips flew as the fallen oak branches were cut into stove lengths.

By the time it came Thad's turn again to rest he wandered off, much to the amusement of Maurice, who knew whither his thoughts must be roving.

Just as he swung the ax above his head for a downward stroke he received an electric shock.

Thad was calling his name, calling in an excited tone, too, as if there was dire need of the other's presence.

"Bring the gun! bring the gun!"

That seemed to be the tenor of the shouts; and as he dropped his tool Maurice swooped up the Marlin, which was standing against an adjoining tree, and jumped for the river bank.

He knew that whatever had happened Thad wanted him at the water's edge; and it was in that direction he hastened as fast as his legs could carry him.

Twice in his haste he fell down, tripping over trailing vines; for the continued shouts of his chum startled him.

And when he burst out of the thicket, to stand on the river bank, close to where Thad was yelling, this was what he saw:

A row-boat was speeding down the river, urged on by the

lusty movements of a red-headed man who was sitting in it; Thad danced about on the deck of the swamp, pointing after the fleeing party, and calling on Maurice to "give him both barrels, the thief!"

But Maurice knew that it was useless, since the other was by this time out of range, and the gun contained only small shot.

Nevertheless, urged on by the frantic appeals of Thad he did level the Marlin, and bang away, though he saw the man duck down before the reports came.

After the bombardment was over the redhead again poked into view, and the fugitive made a movement with his hand to indicate his poor opinion of such useless business.

Maurice, fearing the worst, began to drag the boat in to shore.

Dixie, having been drawn from his prowling around in search of game by the shouts and shots, leaped in even before the little dinghy had reached the bank.

By the time Maurice climbed out on the deck Thad seemed to have recovered from his excitement to some extent.

"Didn't I tell you I saw a face, and wasn't it a sorrel-top, too? Mebbe you'll believe me next time, my boy," he said, impressively.

"Where was he, and what was he doing?" demanded Maurice, showing signs of alarm, and looking a bit weak as he contemplated the grave consequences that might follow this raid.

"In the cabin, of course, and making himself at home. He had his boat on the other side there, so I never suspected anything wrong till he dashed out, jumped into it, and pulled like everything."

"Were you on board then?" asked Maurice.

"Just climbing on deck when he came jumping out like a whirlwind."

"Perhaps you disturbed him in his game then?" suggested Maurice making a bee-line for the open door.

When a few seconds later the other followed him it was to see Maurice on hands and knees before the little opening in the wall of the cabin, thrusting in his arm as far as he could.

"Oh! Thad, it's gone—the thief got away with poor Bunny's money!" he was exclaiming, his voice full of horror.

"Well, he would have hooked it, only for something I did that you'd have called silly if you'd seen me!"

And with this complacent remark Thad coolly walked over to the shelf where some of their cooking utensils stood, took down the battered old coffeepot, and throwing back the lid, thrust his hand inside.

The astonished eyes of his mate followed each little proceeding with rare interest; and when Maurice saw the well remembered diary of old appear, which being opened disclosed the lovely yellowbacks nestling within, he gave a shout twice repeated, while he swung his hat around his head.

"Bully for you, Thad! I take it all back, every word! It surely does pay to be cautious, even if people call you an old woman. Only for that he might have found the money; and then how mean we'd feel. Tell me what you did. He acted like he was satisfied he'd done a big thing."

"Well, perhaps he knows better now, if he's had time to tear open the package I put in place of this book; for it was a nice fat sliver of wood!" laughed Thad.

Thereupon Maurice grappled him with a bear-like hug, and waltzed him out on deck, to the intense delight of Dixie, who seemed to think all this demonstration must be for his benefit, for he set up a furious barking and snapped at the heels of the dancing boys.

When they went ashore again things were left differently. The cabin door was locked, with Dixie inside. They could depend on his snappy barking to give warning of any uninvited guest aboard.

But the wood-cutting proceeded without further alarm.

True, Thad was so nervous over the matter that he insisted on carrying what fuel they had cut down to the dinghy every little while, just so he could call out to the yellow cur, and have him give a reassuring bark.

And finally the several loads had been safely ferried across the watery gap, so that the cruisers were ready to start moving.

The anchor was raised by means of a primitive but effective derrick Maurice had devised. This he also made use of in handling the square fish net which could be dropped over the side, baited, and then lifted half an hour later, with more or less generous results. Of course this method of fishing was only to be enjoyed while they were at anchor. It is in general

St. George Rathborne

use along the Ohio river; and indeed, Maurice had even seen pictures of the same thing in the magazine lying on the table, and which illustrated queer doings far off in Uncle Sam's Philippine possessions.

Once again they were floating southward, with a moving panorama of shore to interest them.

Maurice was figuring on the swiftness of the current, just how many miles an hour it ran at this point, and when they were likely to bring up at Morehead.

"I think we ought to make it by sun-down, Thad," he finally announced, after finishing his complicated calculations.

"You make me feel good, partner, when you say that," returned his chum, who was handling the sweep and keeping the boat a certain distance from the shore, where they could get the full benefit of the current without taking undue risks of being swept out on the broad bosom of the majestic river.

"Yes, I know what's on your mind. You'd like to get rid of our responsibility, and hand that packet over to Bunny," remarked Maurice.

"Wonder what she's like; sounds as if she might be a little girl; but that couldn't be, for she was his daughter," Thad said.

"Yes, and has three kids, the book said. Oh! that must have been a pet name for her when she was little. The chances are well find her a strapping big woman, something like that one we bought our last loaf of bread from."

"Well, she won't take after her pa then, that's all, Maurice."

"Why, was he small," asked the other.

"I always thought so, for a man; not quite as tall as I am; and with a voice like a lady's. I liked old The; and I wish he had only lived long enough to deliver his own money to Bunny," Thad went on.

"I was wondering where that fellow came from, Thad."

"Who, our visitor of last night and this morning? Oh! I suppose he's got a shack somewhere below here, and was on the way home from an up-river town when he sighted our craft, and crept aboard to see if there was anything he could pick up."

"That's about the right thing. Say, I bet he was hopping mad when he tore open that package, and saw what he had drawn in the lottery, eh, Thad?"

"Mad would never fill the bill. I hope he don't wait up for us, and give us a shot or two wlien we sail past his cabin. I'd hate the worst kind to have my skin filled with shot; and nobody could ever prove who did it. That's one reason why I've steered further away from the bank than we generally keep, you notice, Maurice,"

"Well, that's level old head on your shoulders, my boy. The fellow who gets you napping will have to tumble out of bed right early in the morning, I reckon," laughed Maurice, patting his chum patronizingly on the shoulders.

"And I keep one eye on the shore, too, pretty much all the time. Just let me see anybody moving, and I'm ready to drop flat till the storm rolls by. What's that over there right now, Maurice?"

St. George Rathborne

He pointed with quivering finger at some object that seemed to be bending down the bushes on a certain projecting point which they happened to be approaching.

"Don't worry; it's all right. That is only a cow, for you can see her horns from here, Thad."

"But seeing horns sometimes spells trouble. They say the devil mounts a fine pair, you know. A cow, Maurice, means human kind near by; that stands for a cabin; and how do we know but what our sorrel-top friend of this morning owns the ranch. Just lie down behind that box, or go into the cabin till we drift past. I'll feel easier when we leave the thing a mile above."

A hail from the shore presently came floating over the water; but it was a negro who called, and he only wanted to know if they had any coffee they would spare him.

Since their entire stock amounted to just enough for a scant week, with meagre chances for replenishing the caddy when exhausted, since their funds were very low, of course they had to reply in the negative.

The darky was inclined to be talkative, as is usually the case, and even followed them half a mile along the bank, trying to find some basis for a dicker.

"Thank goodness he can't cross that creek!" exclaimed Maurice, as they passed the mouth of quite a good sized stream that flowed into the enormous river, adding its mite to the gigantic flood.

The colored gentleman looked as though it would only require the least encouragement for him to step in and swim across; but as this was not forthcoming he waved his ebony arm in farewell and turned back again.

Thad breathed easier.

Nevertheless, for hours he continued to scan the shore-line ahead; and once, when some unseen hunter fired at some sort of game back from the river's edge, the sweep-tender was seen to duck his head mechanically, much to the amusement of his companion.

The day grew old, and they had made uninterrupted progress, not even stopping for the midday meal. While Thad held the long oar his mate slung some sort of a hot meal together, which satisfied their voracious appetites and warmed them as well.

"Where's your storm?" asked Thad, about the middle of the afternoon, as he glanced up at the sky.

"Here, you're squinting in the wrong direction, man. Suppose you look to the southward, a little veering toward the west. Don't you glimpse some dark clouds there?"

"Of course," Thad agreed; "but that's a poor sign. Why, you can nearly always see some clouds hanging low down there. It's been getting warmed right smart. That sun feels almost hot to me."

"That's a pretty good sign of rain, that seldom fails. But what do we care! Our roof don't leak, Thad!"

"No, but it will be tough if the downpour comes just when we want to look for George Stormways and Bunny. I suppose, though, we could tie up at Morehead and wait till it passes by."

"Hope we haven't passed it already," said Maurice, looking serious.

"Oh! I don't think that could be possible, do you? If the place is big enough to get marked on the chart, it ought to be of a size for two fellows to see it in passing. And the two landings we did notice were other settlements, for we asked their names. One man said Morehead was below a piece. I'm expecting to see it soon."

"Suppose we don't till dark?" remarked Thad, always on the lookout for trouble. "What are you going to do then?"

"Keep right along, sonny, until we see lights, when we can push in and tie up. It's Morehead or bust!"

"All right, you're the skipper, I told you, Maurice. The cook has ideas of his own, but he ain't going to run counter of an experienced navigator like the boss. But I hope we come across that station before dark. You know the moon don't rise till about nine now; so we can count on several hours of black sailing."

Thad said no more, neither did his comrade make any attempt to continue the argument; for both of them were still hoping that Morehead would consent to show up inside of another hour.

But for some reason distances seemed unduly lengthened on this particular day, and the gloaming swooped down upon them with the coveted goal still undiscovered ahead.

Maurice was grimly set upon keeping his word.

As a usual thing they discouraged night traveling on the great river, because of the aggravated perils involved; but this was a case that was out of the common.

Thad went in to look after the wood fire, and wrestle with the problem of what to have with the baked 'possum, that had been cooking much of the afternoon.

There were no sweet potatoes now, since the last one had been devoured on the preceding day; so after mature thought the cook was compelled to put on some "grits," as they fortunately still had quite a little stock of this famous Southern staple, which in the North goes by the name of hominy alone.

He hoped that by the time supper was ready they might have reached their haven; either that, or the determination of Maurice to keep moving have suffered a change. If it were otherwise they must eat one at a time, while the other attended to the sweep, and kept watch and ward.

He had things pretty well along when a welcome shout from the pilot outside came to his ears.

"What ho?" asked Thad, as he thrust his head out of the cabin door.

"Lights ahead on the shore, and I reckon we must be close on that old Morehead," returned Maurice.

"I can hear roustabouts chanting," said the cook, as he bent his ear; "and I bet you that's a steamboat getting wood aboard."

"Wouldn't be surprised. If it is, then that place is Morehead. Perhaps this George Stormways may be in charge of the woodyard. Anyhow I reckon we're going to learn something about him here; and now you see that my idea of keeping right along drifting was the correct one after all."

"I suppose so. I hope the steamer don't take a notion to move off while we're passing. I wouldn't like to take the responsibility of ramming and sinking her, you know, Maurice."

"Get in nearer the shore, and we'll drop anchor above the landing. If we do that we needn't worry, because you see she's bound to lean away from land when she starts. That's the ticket. Get in the push!"

Thad had picked up the pole with which they were able in shallow water to urge the shanty-boat toward the shore; he could reach bottom easily, and under his efforts, as well as the swing of the current, and the inclination of the sweep, the Tramp soon gained an offing in water that was not more than three feet in depth.

The two boys could easily see the exciting scene as a line of black ran on board the steam-boat, each carrying two or more sticks of wood on his head, and keeping rhythmic time to the droning chant which every man joined in.

Lanterns and blazing torches made of fat pine knots lit up the weird scene; and taking it in all, they would not have missed it for considerable.

"There goes the pilot's bell—they're off!" exclaimed Maurice, as the line ceased pouring over the guards of the steamboat; then came a loud and hoarse whistle, after which steam began to hiss and the stern wheel to churn the waters of the mighty Mississippi.

"Now it's our turn," laughed Maurice, prepared to drop down to the landing, where a fire burned and threw a glare around.

CHAPTER XV

THAD GETS A SHOCK

The arrival of the little Tramp did not create anything like the commotion which marked the landing of the big stern-wheel river steam-boat.

A few darkies idling on the shore drew near, filled with curiosity when they discovered that only two boys comprised the crew of the floating craft; and Dixie barked strenuously at them, as if to let the community know that while the shanty-boat failed to possess a whistle, it was not without some means of announcing its arrival.

Thad threw a rope ashore to one of these blacks, who whipped it about a post, and the boat presently lay alongside the landing.

"You go ashore and ask questions."

It was Thad who said this, because he knew his chum was so much better able to probe things than himself.

"All right," replied Maurice, readily, "and you can look after the boat; though likely enough none of these fellows will try to run away with it."

St. George Rathborne

"Well, I don't mean to give them half a chance. Just think what would become of us if such a thing happened. We'd have to go to work on a cotton plantation, sure, to make money enough to get further along. I've got the good old Marlin handy, Maurice, and just let any thief try to come aboard, that's all. I'll pepper his hide for him, and salt it in the bargain," declared Thad, resolutely.

"I believe you would, boy," laughed his comrade, as he stepped from the deck to the shore.

He had already noted that Morehead did not appear to be much of a place. Indeed, beyond the piles of cordwood, and a few scattered cabins, there did not seem to be anything of a settlement.

"Only excuse it has for being on the map is that some steamers find it convenient to stop and wood up here. That woodyard is the whole thing," thought Maurice. He turned upon the negro who had whipped the cable around the post in an obliging way.

"Where can I find the man who runs the woodyard?" he asked.

"'Deed, I reckon he am in hees store dar, boss," came the reply.

"A store, eh? Where is it situated?" continued Maurice, bent on following up the clue.

"See dat flare up yander—dat am de light in de windy. Mars Kim he keep gen'ral 'sortment ob goods. On'y place to buy grits in ten mile," observed the other, pointing.

"What is his name?" asked the boy, deeming it only right that he should be fully armed with this much information before starting in to interview the other.

"Mars Kim, fuh sho'! Dat's wat we allers calls him, boss. Reckons, as how yuh haint gut sech a ting as some terbaccy 'bout yuh, now? I'se done clean out."

Maurice shook his head in the negative.

"I'm sorry, but you see, I don't smoke," he remarked.

He would have willingly tossed the moke a nickel for his readiness to assist them; but truth to tell, even such small coin happened to be at a premium with the voyagers just then—although they carried a small fortune in yellowbacks, not for worlds would they think of making use of a single bill for their own benefit—it was a sacred trust in their eyes.

He strode over to the building where the brilliant light in the window announced headquarters. Closer investigation disclosed the fact that the glow was caused by an acetylene lamp which piece of enterprise doubtless caused the storekeeper to assume a high place in the estimation of the lazy negroes, and shiftless "white trash" of the neighborhood.

It was a general country store.

Maurice had seen many such, though, as this one happened to be at a point much further south than the others, it doubtless contained features that stamped it unique in his eyes.

But they had no money to spend in groceries just then; and it was an entirely different errand that caused him to venture into the establishment.

Over the door he noticed a sign which he was just able to read.

It at least gave him the name of the proprietor.

Store, and Office of Woodyard. Kim. Stallings, Prop.

A gawky clerk, undoubtedly of the "cracker" persuasion, was waiting on several dusky customers, and vainly endeavoring to keep them in a clump, as if he feared to let the bunch scatter, lest certain unprotected articles vanish with their departure.

Looking further Maurice discovered that over in one quarter there seemed to be a sort of enclosure, over which was the significant notice "P. O."

He could see that some one was behind the gaudy brass grillwork; and believing that this was likely to be the proprietor, engaged in entering upon his books that late delivery of cordwood to the steamboat, the boy moved that way.

As he stood there in front of the little opening the man beyond looked up. He seemed surprised to see a stranger.

"Evenin', sah. What can I do foh you?" he asked politely, upon discovering that it was a white person.

"Is this Mr. Stallings?" asked Maurice.

"Yes, sah, that is my name," replied the other, curiously.

"I have just come off a shanty-boat that is tied up here. I have a chum with me on the boat. We want to find a man by the name of George Stormways. Can you tell me if he happens to live near by?"

"Huh!"

The owner of the woodyard and country store bent forward still more and took a closer look at the speaker. It seemed to Maurice as though Mr. Stallings had suddenly become more deeply interested in the personality of the stranger, though he could not give even a guess just why that should be so.

"George Stormways," repeated Maurice, slowly and deliberately, as though he wanted the other to fully understand.

"Why, yes he gits his mail hyah, sah; leastways, he allers used tuh come hyah tuh trade, when he had any money. George worked foh me a long spell, till the shakes knocked him out," said the other, finally.

Maurice had been studying the man. He believed he could see honesty in his thin sallow face, but hesitated to say anything about the real motive that influenced himself and chum to stop in order to hunt up George Stormways.

Such a secret had better be confined to as few persons as possible. Still, that would not prevent him from saying that he had some good news for the man he sought.

"How far away from the Landing does he live, Mr. Stallings?" he asked, promptly.

"Reckons as how it air all o' fo' mile, sah. An' in the present disturbed condition o' the country, mebbe, sah, it would be wise foh you to defer yuh visit thah to mawnin'," came the reply.

"I reckon we'll have to, sir, if we can tie up below the

landing without getting in the way. We want to see George and his wife the worst kind, and couldn't think of going on down the river without making a big effort to do so. Yes, we'll spend a day at Morehead, and get acquainted. I only wish we were better supplied with cash, so we might trade with you; but just now it happens we're on rock bottom."

The other seemed to be fairly consumed by curiosity. Never before had he known such a bright lad to be drifting south on a shanty-boat. Usually those aboard such craft were seasoned river travelers, men who lived on the water, "Mississippi tramps," as they are called, some of whom MIGHT be honest, though he judged the entire lot by the character of a few, and they the worst.

But here was a bright, wide-awake boy, with a face that somehow interested him, despite his inborn suspicion.

"What did yuh say yuh name might be, sah?" he asked.

"I didn't happen to mention it, but it is Maurice Pemberton. We are both natives of Kentucky, and on the way to New Orleans to meet my uncle, who is captain of a big steamer, due there in February."

"Would yuh please step around to the side, an' oblige me by coming in hyah. Seems like I feel an interest in yuh-all, and if yuh felt like tellin' me the story I'd be obliged."

Maurice was only too willing to oblige. At the same time he continued to hold to his resolution to handle the subject of the money with due caution. Mr. Stallings was undoubtedly perfectly trustworthy; but the information might get afoot, and cause trouble.

Of course he could not decline to make a friend of the

storekeeper, who had taken an interest in the voyage of the little Tramp. Maurice was only a boy, but he knew that one could never have too many friends in this world.

So he followed directions, and was speedily seated alongside Kim. Stallings, telling him all about how the voyage happened to begin.

The man became greatly interested as he proceeded and read the wonderful letter from Uncle Ambrose with kindling eyes.

"Glad yuh stopped in hyah, Maurice; glad tuh have met up with yuh; and if so be yuh are short with cash, I wouldn't mind trustin' yuh foh some grits and such like. I reckons sho' yuh'd send the money aftah yuh met with this uncle. So don't yuh go tuh worryin' 'bout gettin' on short rations, my boy," remarked Kim. Stallings, after he had talked with the other for some little time.

"That's awful fine of you to say so, Mr. Stalling. Perhaps we'll take you up, though my chum is against running in debt a cent. But we have a long trip ahead of us yet, and to stop over and go to work to earn money enough to buy grub might keep us from getting down to Orleans in time to meet Uncle Ambrose."

Maurice insisted upon shaking the lean hand of the Dixie storekeeper as he said this, an operation to which the other did not seem in the least averse.

"But yuh said that yuh wanted to meet up with George Stromway the wust kind," continued the man, kindly; "in the mawnin' I'll start yuh right. P'raps one o' his kids might be 'round tuh take yuh through the woods, and 'round the swamps, foh it's ticklish travelin' with a stranger, sah."

"We have some good news for George," admitted the boy.

"Well, now, I'm glad tuh hyah that same. I reckon he needs it right bad around now. Nawthin' ain't a gwine tuh do pore George any lastin' good till he pulls up stakes an' gits outen this low kentry. If he was only on a farm up on higher land I reckon the shakes'd give the critter the go-by. But George, he cain't never raise the money he'd have tuh put up, tuh rent a farm an' buy the stock foh it."

"Would it take very much?" queried Maurice, trying to appear quite unconcerned, though he was really quivering with eagerness.

The storekeeper looked at him and smiled, as though he could read the boy's face like a printed book.

"Oh! not so very much, sah. I done reckons as how a couple o' hundred'd do the trick; but that means a heap o' money tuh a pore feller like George. He done tole me a year back that some relative o' hisn up-Nawth was a thinkin' o' comin' down with some cash, an' settin' o' him up on a farm; but it all seemed to blow over. He was nigh broke up about it, too, sah, I tell yuh."

Maurice could not hold in altogether.

"It was his wife's father, old The. Badgeley. My chum knew him well. He didn't come because he died. But he left something for his daughter. He called her Bunny, and I don't even know her name," he said.

"That sounds real good, sah; and I sure am glad tuh heah it. I've done all I could afford foh George; but he don't seem to hold out. Many times he's kim back to work foh me, an' broke down. It'll be a godsend foh the pore feller, if so be he kin pull out. I'll see that you git a fair start in the mawnin' sah, I shore will."

Maurice began to fear that his chum might be growing anxious about him, so he got up to leave.

"Nothin' yuh-uns 'd like tuh have to-night?" inquired Mr. Stallings, as he shook hands warmly at parting.

Maurice smiled and shook his head.

"There's lots we need," he said; "but I wouldn't dare think of accepting your kind offer without consulting Thad. He's queer about running up debts. But in the morning we'll both see you again."

So he said good night, and went out, resolutely shutting his eyes to the abundance of good things to eat that greeted him on every side.

Thad was eagerly waiting for him, and the other could see that he was brimming over with excitement.

"Say, if it wasn't for wanting to meet up with George so bad I'd be for dropping down river five miles, and giving this beastly old place the go-by," he said, as Maurice came aboard.

"Why, what on earth is the matter?" asked the other, dismayed.

"Then you didn't hear anything about it, eh? I reckon it's such a common occurrence around this part of the country they don't think anything about it," continued Thad, seriously.

"Why, whatever in the wide world are you talking about,

son?" demanded Maurice, greatly puzzled to account for this new evidence of timidity on the part of his friend, who, as a usual thing, had always seemed bold enough.

"I don't like it so close, that's all. I bet you I dream of the thing tonight, and every time I look up it seems like my eyes always went straight there."

He pointed up the bank.

Maurice followed his extended forefinger to a point just a little further along, where some trees stood.

He could see some object that seemed to move to and fro like the exhausted pendulum of a clock.

Apparently it was suspended from a limb, and as Maurice caught the true significance of what his chum meant, he felt a cold chill pass through his frame.

"Say, do you mean to tell me that is a man hanging there?" he asked; and if his voice took on a sudden hoarseness, it was not to be wondered at under the circumstances.

"I just reckon it must be," returned Thad, pleased to note that his comrade seemed just as filled with horror as he himself had been.

"But do you KNOW it is—did any of those coons tell you so?" persisted the other.

"N-no, because, you see, Maurice, I never noticed it when they were around. The moon, managed to climb up while you were gone; and then I just happened to see it. Ugh! I've done mighty little else but stare at it ever since."

"But perhaps you may be mistaken, Thad."

"Sure; but don't forget that we're away down in Dixie, now; where they hang a darky without bothering trying him, if so be he's shot a white man. And don't it LOOK like it—tell me that, Maurice?" went on the late guardian of the shanty boat.

"Oh! I admit that it does, all right. But if you think I'm going to let the whole night go by without investigating this thing, you're away off."

Maurice turned resolutely around as he spoke.

"Where are you going?" demanded his chum, nervously.

"Ashore again to see. If that is a man, I rather think Mr. Stalling would have said something to me about it; though now that I think of it he did hint that it wasn't altogether safe for a stranger to go wandering off into the woods and swamps right now. Perhaps it's just as you say, and this is some black thief they caught. But I hope you're mistaken, Thad."

"I do, too, because you see I want some sleep tonight. But hold on."

"What's the matter now?" asked the other, as Thad caught his arm.

"I'm going with you, that's all," and accordingly he stepped ashore, carrying the gun along with him.

They approached the suspicious object with more or less display of valor; though doubtless the hearts of both lads beat like trip- hammers from the unwonted excitement.

The moon, which had been partly hidden by some fleecy, low-lying clouds, now took a sudden notion to sail into a clear patch of blue sky; and in consequence objects could be much more readily seen.

Both lads strained their eyes to discover how much truth there might be in the grim suspicions of Thad.

Not until they were close up to the strangely swaying object could they fully decide as to its character.

Then Thad gave a grunt, while Maurice laughed.

"That's the way with most ghosts, Thad; when you get close up they just turn out to be something awfully common and you feel sick to think what you imagined," remarked Maurice, as he put up his hand and took hold of the swinging object.

"Say, who'd imagine now that they'd hang up an old bundle of wraps off goods, like this?" said Thad, in disgust.

"But you can sleep all right now," remarked his friend, not a little relieved himself to find that they were not up against one of those grim tragedies that have been so common through the country of the lower Mississippi.

"That's right. Let's get back home. I want to hear what you picked up about George," declared Thad, a little confused.

And accordingly they once more went aboard the boat, seeking the comfortable interior of the cabin, where Maurice could spin his yarn, and a council of war be called to decide on many matters.

CHAPTER XVI

THE TROUBLE THAT WAS MET ON THE ROAD

The night seemed unusually long to Thad.

They had locked the door of the cabin, and by this time he had come to the positive conclusion that no human being could ever climb in through the little window, as long as that stout iron bar remained across its center.

Nevertheless, half a dozen times Thad awoke, and on each and every occasion he seemed to deem it a solemn duty to get out of his bunk, pass over to the window, which was, of course, open for ventilation, and observe the whole of the shore that could be seen.

But the bright moonlight bathed the bank in its radiance, the soft night wind murmured among the trees, and possibly certain sounds, such as the hooting of owls, or the barking of some honest watchdog, disturbed the silence of the night, yet there was no cause for alarm.

Morning came at last.

It had been decided that they might accept the kind offer of the storekeeper to a limited extent. They would be foolish to allow a scruple to stand in the way. Besides, even as it was, they stood to run up against trouble below, from a shortage of provisions.

So Maurice went ashore, and, seeking the store, was cordially greeted by the proprietor.

"Made up yuh mind tuh trade with me, sah?" asked Mr. Stallings, as he thrust out his lean brown hand in greeting.

"We have up to five dollars. My chum refuses to get any deeper in debt. And if you have no objections we'll carry off a slab of breakfast bacon and some grits right now," returned Maurice.

"Right glad you settled it that way. I'd ben sorry tuh see yuh go on without some provisions, sah. Pick out just what yuh want, an' I'll make a note o' it. But if so be ten dollars 'd seem better tuh yuh, don't hang back," went on the generous Southerner.

"I wouldn't dare go one cent beyond the five, or Thad would be after my scalp. And he'll want to see the bill, too, depend on that."

Maurice quickly returned to the boat, bearing the bacon and grits; for without the same their breakfast would have been slim, indeed.

Afterward they locked the cabin, and both ventured over to the general store; for Thad was determined that since the precious packet had to be delivered to George that morning, he was not going to let his chum have all the pleasure of bringing joy into the life of the poor family.

"Besides," he added, when making his plea, "who knows

what trouble you might meet up with on the road? If the storekeeper hinted that it wasn't right safe for strangers to be wandering around, perhaps you might be held up by some thieves. Two would be better than one if that happened, you know."

Maurice was well satisfied that it should be so; though he had not brought the subject forward, he hardly fancied the idea of taking that four mile jaunt and back, alone.

Besides, the possession of so much money was apt to arouse fears that might never have occurred to him otherwise.

So he had readily assented to the proposition of his chum.

Mr. Stallings was pleased to meet the second lad; and Thad quite took to the Southern storekeeper and woodyard proprietor at sight.

They remained long enough to get full directions concerning the road that would bring them to the desolate little home of George.

"I'd advise yuh tuh keep an eye out along the swamp, boys. They's a few bad coons somewhar in that thar place. The sheriff he 'lows tuh git 'em right soon, an' any day weuns hyah 'spect tuh see 'im drift in wid some prisoners. I heard as how he had collected his posse three days back. Keep that gun right handy, son; an' if so be yuh have tuh shoot, make her tell!"

All of which might be interesting news; but it was hardly calculated to quiet the nerves of the two boys.

However, they were not the kind to give up any cherished object simply because it involved peril.

"Thank you, Mr. Stallings. You said you'd keep an eye on our boat while we were gone, didn't you? It isn't much of a beauty, but you see it's all we've got; and we calculate that it'll just have to carry both of us to Orleans," remarked Maurice, as they started away.

"Don't yuh think of any harm acomin' tuh the boat, sah. I'll give yuh my word they wont. And if so be yuh choose tuh stay over night, I'll use the key yuh left with me, an' put a man inside tuh keep guard, a man who would as soon shoot a thief as eat his bacon."

So the two chums started off.

The morning was delightfully fresh, with the sun shining overhead, and just a tank of frost in the air, enough to make them tramp along with a spring to their steps.

But before they had gone beyond the last cabin Thad gave utterance to an ejaculation of dismay.

"What's the matter now; forgot something? Hope the Marlin is loaded, and you picked up a few more shells for your pocket?" said his comrade, as they both stopped short.

"Oh, sure, I saw to all that. It's a different matter," mumbled Thad, who seemed to be staring hard at something to one side.

Turning, Maurice discovered a tumble-down shack, around which several dirty white children were playing.

"What is it?" he asked; "didn't think you saw a ghost, again, eh?"

Thad shook his head.

"Nope. This was a live ghost, I reckon. And he had a fiery red-top in the bargain," he said positively.

Immediately Maurice understood what ailed him.

"A man with a red head of hair; and you think it might be the same fellow that tried to rob us yesterday up-river? Is that it?"

"Sure it is," replied Thad.

"But you know there are lots of men with red hair?" protested his comrade.

"Yes, but not with that nasty laugh. You heard it when he paddled away, thinkin' he had the stuff; and I heard him give the same kind of laugh just when he dodged into that shack."

"He did, eh? Funny I didn't happen to hear it. What made him laugh this time, d'ye suppose, Thad?"

"Ask me something easy, will you? P'raps he was tickled to see old friends again. Then, again, mebbe the notion struck him that after all the fish that got away the other time was comin' straight into his net. All I know is he laughed; and that it's the same critter!"

When Thad was positive it took mountains to change his opinion.

But then Maurice did not see that there was anything improbable in the idea, since the thief who had visited them had rowed down river, and just as likely as not had his home at Morehead.

"Well, come along, pard. Even if it is our old acquaintance,

St. George Rathborne

he'd better think twice before trying to hold us up," he remarked, giving a pull at the other's sleeve.

"But he knows what we've got along. He may tell some others just as tough as himself; and how could we hold up our end if half a dozen tackled us?" grumbled Thad, as he stalked along at the side of his chum.

"Shall we go back, then?" asked the other.

"Nixy. I don't care if there's a dozen coming, we're going to get to George all right. You hear me, Maurice."

"That's the right way to speak. But, after all, perhaps we won't have the least bit of trouble. Didn't you hear Mr. Stallings say the sheriff was abroad with a posse, looking for rascals. Strikes me that this wouldn't be a good time for our friend to try any of his tricks. They use a rope down here for a remedy. Jails are played out. There's no need of bothering any, Thad."

So they walked briskly along the road, which was, after all, not much of a thoroughfare, and required close watching lest they stray away and lose themselves.

But the storekeeper had given plain directions, so that with proper diligence they should not have any trouble about keeping along the right path.

Although Thad had appeared to agree with his chum that there was no need for worry, it might be noticed that he let Maurice do most of the looking for the right signs that were to safeguard their course. On his part he felt that necessity demanded that he twist his head just one in so often and scan the rear.

Maurice knew what he was doing, but made no complaint. Indeed, in secret, he was almost as anxious as Thad, even though he had not seen the man with the red head with his own eyes; and had tried to laugh at the idea of his being the same scoundrel who had tried to rob the shanty-boat further up the river.

After they had placed Morehead Landing some distance in the rear they found themselves in a very lonely place, indeed.

Evidently they must be approaching the swamp spoken of by the friendly storekeeper. Here and there they could see trailing streamers of Spanish moss clinging to the branches of the trees; and the further they went the more desolate their surroundings became.

"Say, ain't it enough to give a feller the shivers?" observed Thad, when an owl began to hoot in a mournful way back from the road.

"I must say it doesn't seem to be particularly cheerful around this region. But we must be more'n half way there; and nothing's happened yet," returned Maurice, stoutly.

"There, what was that?" asked his chum, coming to a sudden stop.

"Where?" demanded Maurice, who had taken his turn at carrying the gun; and as he spoke bringing it half way up to his shoulder, while his thumb played with one of the hammers.

"I saw something moving ahead; sure I did!" declared Thad, shaking that obstinate head of his the whole.

"Perhaps so, but that's not saying it was a MAN! Did it have red hair, do you know, Thad?"

"There you go, Maurice, always making fun of me. I didn't see any head, so I can't say; but it looked like a man creeping off."

"Right where, son?"

"Do you see that clump of bushes, the ones with the bully red leaves? Well, it was close to them. It moved just when I happened to look that way. I give you my word, Maurice."

"All right. We'll find out quick enough, I reckon," remarked the other, with that decisive ring in his voice which Thad knew so well.

"Now what are you goin' to do, pard? Don't be too rash. Remember what Mr. Stallings, said," and Thad laid a restraining hand on his chum's arm.

But Maurice was not to be daunted.

"Fall in behind me, then. I'm going up to the bushes and see for myself what it was. Ten to one it must have been a muskrat out of the swamp; or perhaps a fox, prowling around for his grub."

He cocked both barrels of the Marlin, and the act must have instilled new courage in the heart of Thad, for he immediately removed his detaining hand.

"All right, then; go ahead. If he jumps for you, poke the old gun in his face."

He stooped down and secured possession of a stout cudgel himself, as though he felt inclined to back up his comrade after a fashion.

In this manner they slowly approached the clump of bushes, where the frost had turned the leaves to rusty red color.

Maurice was on the alert for any sign of trouble. He even passed partly around the clump, without discovering anything to indicate the presence of an enemy.

When he had made sure that the bushes did not conceal a lurking figure, he turned to Thad with a grin.

"Went off in smoke, I reckon. A fellow who can see a hanging coon in a bundle of burlap strung up to a tree might imagine anything, it seems to me," he said a little sarcastically.

Thad looked somewhat sheepish.

He allowed his head to droop, and shrugged his shoulders.

"I did see something move, I tell you. It seemed to skip back out of sight, like it didn't want me to get my peepers on it," he said, with a conviction that would not be denied.

"All right. I hear you; but please show me the animal or human being. I'm willing to be convinced, Thad."

The other started to smile.

"I reckon I can't show you the thing that was here, Maurice, but I might do the next best thing," he said, eagerly.

"What's that—point out it's shadow?" jeered the other, still skeptical.

"A smoke ghost don't leave any marks behind, does it?"

"Well, I don't know. I wouldn't like to say, since I never ran up against one. But why do you make that remark, brother?"

"Looky there!"

Thad dramatically pointed down at his feet as he spoke, and Maurice, turning his gaze in that quarter, instantly saw something that caused him to draw in a quick breath and involuntarily clutch the gun with a gesture of alarm.

There were plain marks on the ground, and even as inexperienced woodsmen as the two boys could easily see that these had undoubtedly been made by the big feet of a shuffling man!

CHAPTER XVII

AN UNEXPECTED MEETING

"He was here, all right!" said Thad, in an awed tone, as he looked all around him.

Maurice took several steps forward, as if mechanically starting to follow the plain imprints of those big shoes.

"Hold on, there, pard; you wouldn't want to chase after that critter, now, would you? We haven't lost anybody, that I know about. The best thing for us is to keep right along the road, and mind our own business. Ain't I right?" demanded Thad.

"I reckon you are, son; and don't think I was so silly as to try and follow that creeper. I'm not anxious to see him. Come on, the quicker we get moving the better."

With that Maurice turned on his heel and started off.

"I don't want him to get the notion in his head we're scared about it," he muttered; "but all the same I think we'd better shinny on our own side, and move along."

"Keep that gun ready for business, Maurice," admonished the

other, who flourished his stick in a belligerent way while bringing up the rear.

"Don't you fear about that, my friend. If anybody jumps out at us I'm ready to give him a warm reception!"

Maurice spoke aloud. It was his hope that if the man might be lingering near he would overhear the words, and take warning accordingly.

They hurried along the dimly defined road. It must have been quite some time since vehicles used this, for the marks of wheels were in many places utterly obliterated by the rains of summer and fall.

Three times they really got off the trail; but fortunately their united vigilance told them of the fact before it was too late to remedy it easily.

"Must be getting near George's place," grunted Thad, at last, for he was almost out of breath, what with their haste, and the necessity for keeping that head of his at all angles, so as to forestall any treachery on the part of the enemy, whom he felt sure must be dodging their trail all this time, waiting for a chance to get in a telling blow.

"I'm afraid not. Seems to me Mr. Stallings said it was nearly a mile past the swamp; and you see we've just got to the worst of that."

"All right, then; keep hoofing it, pard. We've just made up our minds that we're going to see George at home, and nothing ain't going to stop us. Get that?" declared Thad.

"Just what I say. Come on again, if you've caught your wind."

Again they pushed on.

Their surroundings seemed even more dreadful than ever; and Maurice realized for the first time what a fearful place a swamp may seem, especially when danger is hovering about, and a hostile figure may spring out from behind any tree.

Even the sudden harsh cawing of a crow that sprang up from the ground and lodged on a branch startled Thad; and when a rabbit bounded away through the brush alongside the road, Maurice involuntarily threw his Marlin half way up to his shoulder as though inclined to press the triggers.

"I hope we left him behind," said Thad, presently, when, for the fiftieth time, he turned his head to look.

"But I don't believe we did," replied the other instantly. "See here, you found that other footprint; what d'ye think of this?"

"He's been here ahead of us, as sure as you live. Oh, look! That little twig jumped up into place right before my very eyes. Don't you see what that means, Maurice? He passed along here only a minute or so ahead of us. That twig didn't have time enough to get back to its position up to now. Phew! Perhaps he's laying for us further on."

"Well, what if he is? Do we go on?"

"Well, I guess yes. Let me carry the shooter now!" said Thad, as he reached out his eager if trembling hand.

"Oh, no! What's the use changing? I'm as fresh as a daisy; and besides, that stick just fits your hand. I'll give him a scare if he tries to jump at us, never fear."

"Just as you say, Maurice; only PLEASE don't get excited

and fill me up with birdshot, instead of the thief."

"No danger, if you keep where you belong, in the rear. There's some pretty suspicious looking trees ahead there, on both sides of the road. We want to watch close now, Thad. Once we get by here, I've a hunch the going may be better."

"Yes," said Thad, whirling his shillalah around in a lively way, as a token of what he meant to do in case of an emergency.

By the time they reached the spot where the trees joined branches across the dimly defined road both boys were in somewhat of a feverish state of apprehension. They looked at each hoary old trunk as if they believed every tree might conceal a crouching enemy, ready to leap out and attack them.

Yet, strange to say, neither of them once thought of craning their necks in order to survey what lay above.

Perhaps, had Thad done so, he might have received more or less of a shock just about that time.

"Hark!" exclaimed Maurice, pulling up.

"That was a shout, wasn't it?" demanded his chum, his eyes seeking those of the other instantly.

"I'm dead sure it was, and not an owl," replied Maurice.

"And it came from ahead there; didn't you think so?"

"It certainly did. Listen, there's more of the same kind. Now what d'ye make of all that?" muttered Maurice.

"Somebody's coming this way, for I can hear the sound of running. Say, perhaps it's the coons he told us about, the outlaws that live in the swamp! Mebbe the sheriff's posse has stirred 'em up like a hornet's nest, and they're on the jump!"

Maurice looked annoyed.

"If that's the case we ought to be hiding ourselves," he declared. "Yes, but just remember, boy, that there's another thing bothering us just now. What if we ran plump into the arms of that red-top who's laying for us?"

"Well, then, let's drop down here behind a couple of these trees. Perhaps they'll go past and never get a peep of us," suggested the one who carried the double-barrel gun.

"No use," chirped Thad, immediately.

"And why not?" asked Maurice.

"They saw us; they know we're here; that's why."

"How do you know that?"

"I just saw a feller bob up along the road there. He swung his arms over his head as he dropped down into another hollow. And look, ain't that some more of the bunch, topping the rise? I tell you, it's all off, Maurice; they've got us caged. Why, we can't run away, and all that's left is to stay here, grin and bear it."

Thad sat down as though he believed it absolutely useless to take the least step toward seeking safety in flight, but, indeed, both of them were already partly winded with their efforts, so that anything in the line of running might be deemed mere madness.

St. George Rathborne

"Hide the packet then, quick! Stick it under that root there, while no one is looking. Perhaps we can fool them yet!" hissed Maurice, as a brilliant idea flashed through his brain.

"Bully for you, my boy! That's the ticket."

While he was speaking Thad drew the small package from his inside pocket, where he had been carefully keeping it since leaving the boat, and with one quick nervous movement thrust the same out of sight under the convenient root.

No sign remained of his action, and he was fain to believe that no human eyes save his own and those of Maurice could have witnessed the act.

But it was not so.

"Say, they're coming on the jump!" exclaimed Maurice, who had remained on his feet while the other squatted, the better to carry out the process of secreting the precious packet.

"How many?" asked Thad, between quick breaths, induced by the tremendous excitement of the occasion.

"Don't know, but a whole lot of 'em. And every mother's son seems to be armed with some sort of gun. A fine chance we'd have against such a husky bunch, if we showed signs of fight. Yet it does go hard against the grain to give up without striking a blow."

Maurice gnashed his teeth and frowned while speaking, fingering the lock of his Marlin nervously.

By this time Thad had risen to his knees, an overwhelming sense of curiosity urging him on.

"Why, Maurice, that's funny!" he exclaimed, immediately

"I don't see it; what's struck you now, Thad?"

"Why, don't you remember what Mr. Stallings told us?"

"Sure I do—that these swamp rats were about as ugly a crowd to handle as he had ever heard tell of; and I guess he was right; for if I ever saw a tough lot of fellow citizens they're coming down on us right now, five, six of 'em. Ugh!" growled Maurice.

"I think you'll live to take that back, old fellow," chuckled Thad, who seemed to be far less alarmed than he had been a brief time previously, though still excited.

"What ails you?" asked the other, querulously.

"Look for yourself. Are those chaps white men or coons?"

"Why, I reckon they all seem to be white, so far as I can see —oh! I declare, I remember now—"

"The storekeeper told us those bad men were niggers!"

"Right; that's what he said. Still, these may be another lot, connected with your friend with the sorrel-top!" declared Maurice, who died hard.

"Rats! You know now just as well as I do that yonder is the sheriff and his posse! Perhaps they think we're some of the riffraff they've been chasing, and that's why they keep aiming their blamed old guns at us that way. Hadn't we better hold up our arms, Maurice, and give 'em to understand that we surrender? Some fool might think it fine to take a snapshot at us and explain afterwards he thought we meant to fight!"

"That's right, Thad; a clever idea. So up you go, my boy."

Maurice, as he spoke, allowed the gun to fall at his feet, and elevated both hands as high as he could get them. Thad hastened to follow suit, and it might be he unconsciously cast his eyes upward at the same instant, as though eager to see just how his chum held his.

A sudden spasm seemed to shoot through the frame of Thad, and his companion heard him give utterance to an exclamation; but being so intensely interested in the coming of the runners, who were now very close, he made no comment, nor did he ask questions.

The men quickly closed in around them.

Maurice realized that what his chum had guessed must surely be the truth. He even decided which of the six was the sheriff; for the storekeeper at Morehead Landing had described this individual to him, so that he might know him if they ever met.

"Hello, Mr. Jerrold! Glad to meet up with you, sir. Mr. Stallings told us you were out after some game. But he said it was black meat you wanted, not white," sang out Maurice, cheerily; and when he chose to make himself agreeable the young Kentuckian could win over nearly any man.

"Seems like yuh know me, youngster. Who-all be yuh, anyhow, and what yuh doin' thisaways. I'd like tuh know right well?"

But the sheriff had at the same time made a motion to his men, and all show of weapons vanished. He knew that there was no need of violence in this case.

Maurice quickly told him who they were, and that, desiring to see George Stormway, bearing good news from the North, they had been directed along the road by the friendly storekeeper.

"Don't s'pose now, boys, yuh seen anything o' a pair o' black sheep? We done skeered 'em up outen the swamp, an' when our dawgs gits heah we s'pect tuh track 'em down once foh all," observed the sheriff, now apparently ready to shake hands with the two voyagers.

"No; we haven't met a single person, black or white, on the trail; but we have reason to believe that there's a man hiding around here who wanted to waylay us and rob us."

Thereupon, as the sheriff asked the reason he had for believing such a thing, Maurice started in to explain. He told of finding something of value on the boat that belonged to George Stormway's wife, Bunny Badgeley that was—how the man with the red-top had tried to steal the packet and was baffled by reason of Thad's cunning trick; how his chum had seen him just outside the hamlet of Morehead Landing, the tracks on the road, and finally the figure seen by the clump of bushes.

"Yes," broke in Thad just then, and his chum saw that an expansive grin covered his face as he spoke, "and if the gentlemen will only take a squint up over their heads they will see the party in question squattin' on that limb right above us, where he hid himself, I reckon, thinkin' to just drop down on whichever held the gun!"

Then there was an immediate craning of necks; and loud laughs from the members of the Mississippi sheriff's posse attested to the fact that they had discovered what strange fruit that live oak bore.

CHAPTER XVIII

THE GREAT GOOD NEWS

"It's a big fat 'possom!" shouted one of the posse, swinging his gun upward, as though getting ready to shoot."

"You're away off, Dexter; look closer and you can see the ringed tail of a 'coon!" jeered a second.

"If we had the dawgs hyah we'd have a heap o' sport, gents; but as it is, I reckon as how we'll jest have tuh fill him full o' lead, an' let her go at that!" exclaimed a third member of the party.

These various remarks, while evidently spoken in a spirit of levity, aroused strenuous opposition above. There was an immediate movement of the object straddling the limb. Then two arms waved vigorously, and a high-pitched voice sounded:

"Hold on, thar, yo-uns! I ain't a 'coon, but I'm acomin' down right smart, all the samee. Don't let loose on me, boys; I ain't wuth the powder. I jest wants some un tuh kick me for bein' sech a fool as tuh think you-uns was thet bunch o' swamp-hiders!"

St. George Rathborne

The speaker slid along the limb to the body of the tree and began to make his way toward the ground.

Maurice looked at Thad, and there was perplexity in his eyes. He understood the sly tactics of the red-headed man, and wondered whether they would succeed in hoodwinking the sheriff and his posse.

The question was soon answered, for hardly had the cracker reached the ground than Sheriff Jerrold stepped up to him, that piercing eye fastened on the ugly face of the climber.

"Yer under arrest, Jeff Corbley!" he said, making a motion to one of the others to bind the fellow.

"Me? What fur, sheriff? I declar I jest clim' thet tree 'cause I was skeered. I hed a squint o' yer crowd acomin' over the rise, an' I spected 'twar them coons hustling out fur grub. They got it in fur me, an' I jest het up ther tree quicker nor lightnin'."

But the sheriff was not so easily deceived.

"What's this yer grippin' in yer hand, Jeff? A rock big enough to knock a man silly. Thought tuh drap in down on the head o' this hyah youngster, didn't yuh? Easy way tuh git the upper hand o' him, yuh spected. Shucks! Don't yuh open that mouth o' yourn tuh say another word. We been watchin' yuh a long time, Jeff, an' this time yah make tracks outen the county, OR PAY THE FREIGHT!"

The sheriff made a suggestive motion with his hand in the direction of his neck. Evidently the red-headed man understood.

"Oh, I'll go, all right, sheriff. I kinder hed a sneakin' notion fur a long time thet yuh hed it in fur me. How long do I git?" he whined, as his hands were bound fast behind his back.

"We'll give yuh jest twelve hours arter we git tuh Morehead. Ef so be yuh ain't outen the county by then it's touch an' go with yuh. A hundred dollars tuh the man as draps yuh," remarked the official, with a dreadful calmness.

"Twelve hours is a might short time tuh do it hin, sheriff; but I'll make the try, sho. I'm sick o' this place, anyway."

"And the place are sure sick o' you, Jeff; so it's even all 'round," replied the sheriff, turning his back on Jeff.

The two boys had listened to these little pleasantries with mingled feelings. It was really the first time they had ever been so close to a possible tragedy, and when they found that these grim men did not mean to hang the wretched Jeff both breathed easier.

He had been something of a thorn in their flesh and doubtless was an evil bird whichever way he might be looked at; still, they had no desire to see him meet such a terrible end.

"I heard the dawgs along over there, Kurnel," remarked one of the posse, just about this time.

The sheriff brightened up immediately. He had evidently set his mind on the job of cleaning up the band of black thieves who had for so long a time sheltered themselves in the swamp, and preyed upon the neighboring planters; and the coming of the dogs promised to add to the chances of ultimate success.

"Then we must be hiking, boys. Glad tuh have met you both, an' wish yuh all success. If so be as yuh say, theys some

St. George Rathborne

good news foh George, jest congratulate him foh me, will yuh? He's a good feller, George is, an' has heaps o' friends hyahabouts."

He shook hands gravely with each of the boys, after which Sheriff Jerrold started along the dimly defined road. The prisoner, Jeff, was in the middle of the squad, and did not manifest any great enthusiasm about hastening away; but being a victim of circumstances he just had to run when his captors chose.

Maurice looked at his chum and laughed.

"Say, wasn't that the funniest thing ever?" he exclaimed. "Just to think of that scamp settling himself up there among the leaves of that tree, intending to jump us unawares!"

"Yes," observed Thad, with a shrug of his shoulders, "and he meant to drop that big dornick on your head, because you had the gun. Then, while I was stunned with surprise, I reckon he expected to let go and jump me. I'm not a bit sorry that Jeff is going to get his medicine. If ever a man's face told his character his does. And ten to one he's a big bully, and a wife beater, at home."

"But how did you happen to get on to his trick, for it was you who first discovered him sitting there, and told the rest?"

"Well," said Thad, reflectively. It just happened, that's all. When you said how we ought to hold up our hands—"

"Hold on; it was you spoke about that same thing first," corrected his chum.

"Well, you were the first to do it, and when I followed suit, seemed as if my eyes followed my hands up like I wanted to see that I did it the same as you. That was the luckiest thing ever, for you see I just happened to spy him move his leg. Looked like he was kind of afraid that he might be seen, and was hitchin' along to get behind more leaves."

"But you didn't say anything right away, Thad?"

"Just couldn't, that's why; I was so knocked slabwise and full of laugh. But I knew I ought to let that sheriff into the secret, 'cause he was so mighty anxious to grab some feller. So I opened up. My! But didn't Jeff come down quick?" and now Thad chuckled over the recollection of that hurried descent.

"He just had to; because, you see, he was afraid all the time one of the boys might take a notion to shoot. But as the thing is all over, suppose we shove along," suggested Maurice.

"Good. My mind is easy now, with that sneaker out of the way. What d'ye suppose Jeff meant to do?" asked the other, as he fell in at the side of his chum when Maurice started off.

"Rob us, that's clear. He saw that money, all right, when he peeked in at the window of the shanty-boat, and was wild to get it. Then, after his bully little rush when we were ashore, to find that he had been fooled made him madder than a wet hen; and this time he wanted to make sure."

Thad drew a long sigh, but made no answer. His thoughts were doubtless serious enough, as he recollected that heavy stone which Jeff had not dared drop while descending from the tree; also the ugly look of the desperado's face.

Just as Maurice had predicted, the country began to assume a more cheerful appearance after they had left the swamp behind. It was not long before they came to a cabin, where the smoke was rising above the low roof and several dirty-faced children played before the door, where several lean hogs were grunting in the mud.

"Is this George's place?" queried Thad, in some dismay; for somehow he had been mentally picturing a far different scene.

"I reckon not. I was told that his wife was a superior woman, who once on a time used to teach school. She wouldn't be apt to let her youngsters look like this, even if money was scarce. Wait up, and I'll put the question."

Maurice approached the door. A yellow dog began to bark furiously, the three children ran like frightened sheep, since they seldom saw strangers there, and immediately a slatternly looking woman with the customary thin face of the "poor white trash" of the South made her appearance at the door.

"There's a snuff-dipper for you," said Maurice in a whisper to his chum, as he noted the signs about the mouth of the squatter's wife.

The woman was surveying them with wonder, and not a little awe.

"We want to find George Stormway's place; can you tell us how far along it lies?" asked the boy, politely.

It was wonderful how her tired face brightened up. Perhaps she had not heard such a pleasant voice for ages; and dim echoes of some far off past had been awakened.

"Sho I kin, stranger. It be the second house 'long. Hyah, Danny, yuh gwine tuh show these hyah gentlemen the Stormway place. Git a move on yuh, now, er I'll peel the hide from yuh back, sho. Yuh see," she added, turning once more to the visitors, "Danny, he's ben over tuh take his lesson from Missus Stormway once a week. He kin read tuh beat the band. Git erlong, Danny, an' yuh 'member what I sez!"

Of course there was no necessity for a guide, since they were so near their destination. Maurice believed he could understand the motive that influenced the woman of the house—she hoped these strangers might be liberal enough to bestow a nickel upon Danny for his services; and possibly her stock of snuff was running low.

But they were so glad to know that the journey was nearly over that they made no objection. Maurice believed he could spare a nickel to square accounts.

Danny trotted on ahead. He was a shy little chap, barefooted, of course, and with a ragged shirt and baggy trousers that had evidently been made from a gunny-sack.

Maurice happened to have an old newspaper in his pocket, which contained a few illustrations. It might serve the budding genius as a means for advancing his reading abilities; and so he called Danny back, to present it to him, at the same time also handing over the coveted coin.

For they had passed another shack, where the squalor was even more positive than in the former case, and come in sight of George's home.

"Bully!" Thad could not help saying, as soon as his eager eyes alighted on the little cabin.

Maurice understood just how he felt; indeed, he was experiencing the same sense of relief; for the sight of filth and poverty combined is a terrible thing.

But the Stormway cabin was different. Everywhere could be seen evidences of a woman's hand. Flowers adorned the beds in front, and in the rear there were vegetables calculated to give the family many a meal.

Here, as everywhere, a couple of dogs barked in noisy greeting; but to the boys even these yellow curs seemed of a different breed from those guarding other shacks where poverty abounded.

And while the three children playing before the door were barefooted and had soiled faces, still, as Thad expressed it, this was "clean dirt," by which he meant that they undoubtedly must have accumulated it inside of an hour or two, for there was abundant evidence that water was freely used at this place.

Eagerly the boys waited to see what the daughter of old The. Badgeley looked like. No woman could stand such a life of care and want without showing the lines on her face; but when she came to the door to see what all the racket meant, Thad just threw up his hat and let out a genuine whoop, he was so glad.

Even in her cheap calico dress the woman showed her caliber. Dirt and Mrs. Stormway evidently were at daggers' points, and could not live peaceably together under the same roof. It was a relief just to look at her face, after what they had recently seen.

And when she talked, while there was the Southern accent to some extent, they missed that twang and peculiar type of expression so common among the poor whites.

"This is Mrs. Stormway, I reckon?" said Maurice, as he came up.

"Yes, that is my name, sir," she replied, while her face lighted up with some sort of expectancy.

"My name is Thad Tucker, and I'm from Kentucky, ma'am!"

"Oh! Thad Tucker! Then you are the boy father used to write about? What on earth brings you away down here? Have you come to see me?"

She was holding his hand now, plainly excited.

A man had followed her to the door. He was white and thin, but had a face that Maurice liked at first sight. If this was George, as he believed, then it was worth while that they go to all this trouble to bring him good news.

"This is my friend, Maurice Pemberton. He's from old Kentucky, too. You see," said Thad, hardly able to phrase a connected story in his excitement, "the folks he was livin' with broke up, and he was left with nary a home. Now, I'd been keepin' house on the shanty-boat old The.—I mean your father, give me when he was carried off to the hospital. Maurice he got a letter from his Uncle Ambrose, telling him to be in New Orleans in February, and he'd give him a berth on the big tramp steamer he's captain of. So Maurice and me we made up our minds to drift down South on our shanty-boat."

"And on your way you determined to stop over and see me. How good of you, Thad Tucker. Oh, I am so glad to see you! Now I can hear about my poor father's passing. All I know was contained in a short letter from the authorities of the hospital, saying he had been taken there and died. There was money enough found on his person to pay for burying him, but that was all. Come here, George, I want you to meet my father's young friend, Thad Tucker. You remember reading about him."

The thin man advanced with rather tottering steps, but a pleasant smile on his face. Maurice wondered whether what Kim. Stallings had said would prove true; and if this man, racked by malaria, could regain his health if he changed his home to higher ground.

"But you see I didn't know where you were all this time, only that it was somewhere down South. It was only the other day that, just by some luck, I happened to be hunting a lost trap, when I found something that told us where you lived," explained Thad, fumbling in his pocket.

"And," went on Maurice, taking up the story where his chum faltered, "as we were only a short distance up the river from Morehead, we made up our minds that we must meet with Bunny."

"And give her this," with which words Thad fished out the packet and thrust it hurriedly into the woman's hands.

"Oh, what is it?" she asked, beginning to tremble, not with fear, but delicious eagerness and anticipation.

"Something your dad wanted to get to you. He tried to tell me about it just when he was took, but I couldn't understand him. It was lyin' in a hole back of the lining of the boat, and just where he kept the few muskrat traps he owned," finished Thad.

Mrs. Stormway began to undo the string, though her hands trembled so she could hardly make much progress. Finally George himself had to take possession and cut the cord with a knife.

When he opened the little rusty covered diary and those beautiful yellowback government gold notes fluttered to the ground there was a tense silence. Both George and his wife could not believe their eyes. Perhaps, to tell the truth, they had never before seen even one yellowback note, and hardly understood what they were.

"There's just three hundred and thirty dollars, all in good gold bills issued by the United States Government. And he meant it for you, ma'am, 'cause he says so in his diary. I reckon he wanted to fetch it down when he came in the winter; but he never made the ripple."

While Thad was explaining in this manner George and Maurice were picking up the precious bills. The man was so excited he could hardly speak; but when he stood there with the little book in his hand, he looked at his wife and she at him. Then they rushed into each others' arms, while the boys winked hard to keep the tears from flowing. It was an affecting sight, indeed.

"Now we can get away from here. Now we can go on a farm in the uplands, where you will get strong and well, George. Oh, I am so happy I hardly know what to do! And to think that father saved all this money for me! And that you brought it to us, just when it looked so dark that even I was beginning to be afraid!"

Before Thad knew what she meant to do George's wife was kissing him, and George shaking his hand furiously. Maurice came in for a second edition of the grateful couple's thanksgiving; but on the whole both boys stood the ordeal fairly well.

"Come in and rest yourselves, my dear boys. You have brought me blessed news today, and I shall never forget it;

never. You must stay over night with us, because there is so much I want to know about him. We haven't much to offer you in the way of food, but George here can borrow Captain Peek's mule and go to the store for things."

"Not for us," said Maurice, decidedly; "we will be only too glad to stop over with you one night, since you insist, for, of course, there is lots my chum can tell you. And, by the way, Mr. Stallings sent this package to Mrs. Stormway. I think it's got some coffee in anyhow, for we smelled it. He knew we had some good news for you, and wanted to say that he was mighty glad George would have a chance to pull up stakes and get out of this lowland."

The package did contain several articles in the line of groceries, which the good-hearted storekeeper judged the Stormways would be out of, and when she saw this evidence of his thoughtfulness the eyes of George's wife filled with tears, even though she laughed and appeared light-hearted.

CHAPTER XIX

ONCE MORE AFLOAT

The balance of that day and the evening would long be remembered by the boys. Maurice found the three children bright and interesting; nor was that to be wondered at when they had so intelligent a mother to guide them along the way.

George had considered the future so often, in case he ever had the chance to get on an upland farm, that he had his plans all laid out.

He looked ten per cent better by the time night settled in around that little shack in the wilderness, and even doubting Thad made up his mind that George was going to get well.

And that night was one of pleasant intercourse. There were scant rations in the cabin, but then Bunny knew how to cook, and what they had was a treat to the boys, accustomed to looking after themselves so long. The hoe cake was browned just right and tasted better than anything the boys had eaten for a long while, and somehow the coffee was better than they had been able to brew.

In the morning George took the boys aside.

St. George Rathborne

"I'm agoin' to ask you boys to do me a great favor," he said, mysteriously.

Maurice looked at Thad and the latter turned white. He feared that George meant to insist upon their sharing his little pile, and neither of them would have touched one cent on any account.

"Yes, what's that, George?" asked Maurice, who on second thought remembered that that subject had been threshed over on the preceding night, when the good woman had tried to make them accept a gift to help them along and they had firmly declined.

"Why, you see, I'm that afraid of bein' robbed now that it worried me a heap. Suppose I jest hold out that odd thirty and let you take the three hundred over to Kim Stallings to keep for me till I want it? I'd be mighty much easier in my mind, boys, if you would oblige."

Thad waited for his chum to say, for in a ease of this kind he always deferred to Maurice as being better able to decide.

"To be sure, we will, George; I didn't want to mention it to you, but was a little afraid something might happen to the money. Are you able to leave home today? Could you borrow that mule you spoke of and go with us to Morehead? It would be better to get some paper from Kim to secure you?"

George thought he could make the journey, especially with the mule. And besides, there were some things he would dearly love to fetch back with him—things that Bunny had long gone without, for the boys had seen that she was barefooted.

So it was arranged, to the delight of the good woman and the three young Stormways. This had been a great event in the lives of the boy and two girls, and they never wearied of hanging about the young fellow who had known "mon's daddy."

The mule was borrowed from the obliging neighbor, and about nine in the morning they started for Morehead, George being mounted on the back of the animal, though he tried to insist upon their taking turns.

But at this both boys laughed in scorn. Why, that five miles would only be a "flea bite," as Thad declared, to them; and they really needed the exercise, after being cooped up so long aboard the little old Tramp,

Bunny saw them depart with considerable emotion. Thad was afraid she would insist on kissing him again, but the good woman contented herself with squeezing his hands and telling him once more what a blessing he had brought to her poor little home.

George was interested in the tree that had contained such queer fruit, and as they halted under its branches for a brief spell the boys had to relate the story over again.

They had reached a point nearly two-thirds of the way to the river hamlet when they heard a great barking and baying of dogs. The sound appeared to come from over beyond the big timber.

"Seeds like the sheriff he's barking up the tree at last. I jedge he's got them coons separated from ther hook in the swamp, an' if that's so they ain't agoin' to 'scape him this time," remarked George, as they stopped to listen.

The sounds grew fainter, however, showing that the chase must be leading away from the road they followed.

"I'm right glad of that," remarked Thad, "for d'ye know, Maurice, I'd sure hate to see any more prisoners in the hands of that posse."

"Reckon there wouldn't be much danger o' that," remarked George, with a significant nod, which Maurice took to mean that if caught those black criminals might meet with a short shrift.

He could hardly believe that, however, since Sheriff Jerrold was a duly authorized officer of the law and sworn to see it carried out in the proper manner.

They arrived at the river before noon.

"There she is!" exclaimed Thad, eagerly pointing, and George saw that it was a little squatty shanty-boat he meant.

"Why, I hope you didn't think anybody would be so mean as to steal our Tramp?" demanded Maurice, although he, too, experienced more or less lively satisfaction to once more set eyes on the clumsy craft that had so long been their home.

"Well, down in this country nobody can tell. They say that if a man does anything wrong his first idea is to hook a boat, no matter what kind, the nearest he can lay hands on, and cut downstream. But the sheriff is stirring things up just now, and bad men must lie low. Anyhow, there's our bully old Tramp, right side up with care."

Kim Stallings was glad to see George again, and when he heard what glorious luck had befallen him, there was genuine warmth in the handshake he thrust upon the weak man.

Of course, he was only too willing to act as custodian for the three hundred dollars, and gave George a receipt for the money. When he had settled on the upland farm he meant to rent, he could easily get what the store-keeper was holding for him.

And now it was high time our boys once more started on their voyage.

Hundreds of miles still separated them from their destination, and no one could prophesy what difficulties must be faced and overcome before they eventually brought up in New Orleans.

It was just noon when they let go and pushed out upon the friendly bosom of the mighty Mississippi.

Kim and George gave them a parting salute, which the voyagers sent back with a good will. Then shortly a bend cut them off from view, and the little episode was numbered with the past.

"Anyhow, it was a bully time we had there," said Thad, as he started to knock some sort of lunch together, while his chum looked after piloting the boat.

"You bet it was, and neither of us will ever forget it. When Bunny and Greorge saw that bunch of yellow boys, didn't they stare though? I came near blubbering myself, honest, Thad, I was that worked up," confessed Maurice, frankly.

"Oh! I slobbered right over, only you didn't see me, because I got behind. I'm right glad we did it; and wasn't that a hunky-dory find, though? Every time I set eyes on that hole I'll just have to think of the great luck we had."

The old life was taken up again. Borne along on the rapid current of the powerful river, they made mile after mile as the day wore on.

Nothing of moment occurred to disturb the serenity of the scene, and as evening approached they hunted as usual for a good place where the shanty-boat could be tied up for the night.

Once they thought this had been found when what seemed to be the mouth of a stream was sighted ahead; but as they pushed in it was only to find that another floating family had pre-empted the place.

The boys might have even remained had they seemed to be anything like Bob Archiable, for instance, the clock mender of earlier days, but the looks of the three men they saw quite discouraged them.

"Out we go again," muttered Maurice, as they cleared the mouth of the creek, followed by shouts from the owners of the other craft, who called to them to pull in and "have a good time."

Our boys knew only too well what that implied, for liquor and cards must form the sum total of what these rough characters called a "good time," and they wanted none of that.

So it was just about dark before they found a chance to tie up to a friendly tree that chanced to be close enough to the edge of the bank to take their short cable.

Supper was prepared as usual. The provisions secured from the warm-hearted storekeeper of Morehead Landing enabled them to spread themselves to some extent. And Thad declared that life was worth living again, as he sat there after eating, and lighted his pipe for a smoke.

"What so sober about, Thad?" asked the other, when he had been watching his chum's face for some little time.

Thad looked up, and grinned in his usual happy way.

"Oh! it ain't that I'm feeling bad, for I reckon if any feller has a right to call himself lucky that's me. Where would I be now if it hadn't been for you inviting me to make this cruise—"

"Here, don't you get to harping along like that again, my boy. Didn't you promise to call it square? And do you suppose for one little minute that I'd be here unless you were? Why, in the first place the boat belonged to you. I didn't have half enough money to take me all the way to Orleans; and I just reckon I'd had a tough deal trying to negotiate more, the way things went at our home town. Now, just what were you thinking about? I bet I can give a guess."

"Well, what?" demanded Thad, quickly.

"It wasn't about George and Bunny, because then you'd have had a smile on that face of yours. Seems to me you must have been wondering if they got 'em!"

"Meanin' the coons of the swamp? Yes, that's what I had on my mind. I never saw one of 'em, and yet somehow I keep a-wonderin' whether they had a square show. Oh! well, it ain't any of our business; and I reckon they must've been a bad lot, from what Kim said. But I'm right glad they didn't get 'em while we happened to be there, Maurice."

"That's me, every time. But forget it, and let's talk about what we expect to do down below. Here's the charts, such as they are, and none too reliable at the best. We ought to study 'em time and again, because we may want to take a cut-off and save twenty miles or more."

"Don't they say that's dangerous work?" asked Thad.

"Well, yes, it is, sometimes; but there are several places where all the drifters pass through. You know our bully good friend. Bob Archiable, marked two on the map. He's used 'em several years in succession, he said."

"Yes, that's so; but seems to me he said we'd better keep our eyes and ears open all the way down, and ask questions. Sometimes these cut-offs fill up, and then a shanty-boat gets lost in a heap of cross canals. He says they're like hen tracks sometimes."

"Well," remarked Maurice, thoughtfully, "it would be a pretty tough deal if WE ever got mixed up in one of those puzzles. We're short of grub, and there's only a few dozen shells left. Yes, I reckon we will go mighty slow about leaving the old creek and dipping into any of these tempting canals."

So they chatted and exchanged views as they sat there until both grew sleepy, when the cozy bunks coaxed them into retiring.

Nothing occurred to annoy them during the night; though once Thad awoke suddenly and sat up with a low cry on his lips.

Maurice never heard what the nature of his dream might be; but he could give a good guess and felt that it must in some way be connected with those fugitive blacks of the swamp, and the coming of that sheriff's posse with the fierce dogs.

In the morning they were early astir.

It seemed as though they had been away from home a long time after that one night spent with the Stormways. Thad remarked how natural it was to get breakfast again; and Maurice said something along the same lines as he went ashore to gather up a supply of firewood for future use.

Again they moved with the current, always heading south. Every mile passed over counted, since it took them nearer the point for which they were aiming.

Thus several days glided along.

Bad weather alternated with good, but they were wise enough to prepare in peace for war; and thus did not get caught napping when trouble descended upon them.

As the days passed they talked less and less of what had gone by, and began to take a keener interest in what lay ahead.

Now and then the little old Marlin was called on to supply them with a game supper; and never did it fail to do its duty when the chances were right; so that, on the whole, they fared pretty well, and had no complaint coming.

When two weeks had passed since that night with George Stormways and his family, they were down in the neighborhood made famous during the Civil War; for Vicksburg lay not more than ten miles ahead.

They had been wonderfully favored during this time, and no accident had occurred to mar the run, the weather being on the whole fair, though one cold storm caught them unprepared and gave them a bad night.

That was a time when Thad's prophecies failed to save them from inconvenience; but those who endeavor to read the weather are not bothered by an occasional upset in their calculations, and on the very next occasion he came to time just as smiling as ever.

The river seemed to be growing with each passing day, and stretched so far into the west that there were times when they could dimly see the opposite bank, which Maurice declared must be ten miles distant; though again it would not be anything like that to the Arkansas shore.

But they had now passed the southern border of the state, and he announced that the land they were gazing at far over the tumbling waters was that of Louisiana, the very state for which they were bound.

From this time on they could not expect to make such good progress, because of the unusual care that must be taken in order to keep them from losing themselves in one of the false channels.

Again and again would they be tempted to shorten their day's trip by cutting into one of these enticing necks; but Maurice had resolved that he would not allow such a thing, and in the end it proved a wise precaution.

He believed that an ounce of prevention was better than a pound of cure, as it certainly is under all circumstances, and especially during a water voyage down such a treacherous stream as the Mississippi.

They began to have adventures with strolling darkies who visited them after they had tied up for the night; and once when a noisy crowd had threatened to do them bodily harm because the boys had declined to make them a present of tobacco and strong drink, both of them had to do guard duty during the night for fear of an attack.

All these things told them that they were now getting down into the sunny South, and that they would meet with disappointments there as well as in other places, for true it is things seem more alluring at a distance. But both boys were sturdy in body and determined in spirit, so that they were not apt to be discouraged by a few backsets of this character.

CHAPTER XX

ON A PLANTATION IN DIXIE LAND

Once below Vicksburg and the two boys felt that they were doing well.

True, many difficulties had arisen to give them a chance to show their grit and backbone. Maurice was of the opinion that they had come out of these conflicts with flying colors, and each victory seemed to renew their self confidence, as though that were the true reason for the encounter.

There was no lack of shooting in this region, for ducks traded between the river and adjacent lagoons at all hours of the day, and many times Maurice was able to bring down a feathered pilgrim of the air with a shot from the deck of the shanty-boat itself, retrieving the same with a nail fastened to the end of one of the poles.

What interested the boys most were the cotton fields that they began to see.

Of course, both were familiar with cotton: in many of its aspects, having been born and brought up close to the Kentucky border; but these big fields where they could see myriads of the open bolls not yet culled, late as the season was, caused them much pleasure.

And the negroes became more jovial the farther south they went. It seemed as if the black man in migrating north left his natural condition behind, and assumed many of the cares of the white man. Down in the cotton country he was at his best, full of laughter, careless of tomorrow so long as he had a dime in his ragged trousers, and of course light-fingered when he saw a chance to lift anything and no one appeared to be looking.

The boys had a lot of fun with some of these good natured darkies who came about the fire they were accustomed to starting on shore when the occasion allowed.

Sometimes they bribed them to dance a hoedown, or sing songs as the spirit moved.

Maurice was surprised to find that they favored the sentimental songs of the day, such as were being sung in the North. He wondered so at this that finally he asked one fellow, a gray- headed old chap, what had become of the negro melodies once so famous, and now so seldom heard.

Then he learned that the negro of the South had reached a stage of progress wherein he did not wish to be reminded of the fact that he was once a slave and the property of a white master; and as most of those dear old songs are along that line he gives them the go-by when choosing his minstrel lays.

But by a little species of bribery they managed to induce some of their visitors to sing the "S'wanee Ribber," "Massa's in de Cold, Cold Groun'," "Black Joe," and others of a similar nature.

"Dear Ole Hom'ny Corn" seemed to be a prime favorite among them, and the boys themselves never tired of joining in the chorus.

After they had lost several articles from some of these blacks pilfering they learned to keep the cabin door locked when going ashore. If bent on stealing, the southern negro can accomplish his purpose in spite of watchful eyes, since there will come a moment when attention is directed in another quarter, and like a shadow he will creep aboard and accomplish his end.

Another thing began to trouble them about now, and this was the fact that their slender stock of money had entirely given out, with some weeks ahead before Uncle Ambrose could be expected to come to the rescue.

Hence it became necessary that they find some means of earning something.

Thad could fall back upon his experience as a carpenter, and if he could get employment now and then might bring in enough of the needful to supply them with the necessities of life.

Maurice on his part would only too willingly have done anything in his line if he could find a chance. He was a pretty fair bookkeeper, but it did not seem likely that he would run across any one in this part of the country who wanted his books balanced.

Still both of them began to be on the lookout for opportunities, determined to do whatever their hand came in contact with.

It was at Gibson's Landing that Thad struck his first chance.

Things were getting rather low, and they had not enjoyed a cup of coffee for two days, on account of a lack of supplies or the wherewithal to purchase the same.

Maurice was cleaning some fish they had taken that day when he saw Thad coming at an unusually swift pace, and a look on his face that spoke volumes.

"And now what!?" he demanded, as his partner sprang aboard.

"Bully news—I've struck a job. Last a week or so, and give us enough cash to carry us through with careful nursing. And that ain't the whole of it, either," was the way he broke loose.

"It's good as far as you've gone; now what else can there be to make you feel so fine!" demanded Maurice.

"Mr. Simon Buckley—"

"Who's Mr. Simon Buckley?"

"Why, I was just going to tell you—he's a rich planter back here a bit. I happened to mention the fact that I was a carpenter looking for a job and he jumped on to me and said he was looking for just such a man."

"Hurrah!" broke in the other, his face full of smiles.

"Then we got to talking," Thad continued, "and I told him all about what we were trying to do, and he seemed interested and asked questions, principally about you. What d'ye think; he knows your Uncle Ambrose; why once, many years ago they were together in Cuba? And he wants both of us to come with him tomorrow when he starts back to his home; because he says he's got his books in a terrible muss, and would be mighty glad to have you straighten 'em out; and what d'ye think of all that, eh!"

Maurice smiled at his enthusiasm, but was certainly feeling a bit the same way himself.

"Why, all I can say is what you're so fond of shouting whenever any good luck floats our way—bully, bully, bully all around! I felt sure we'd strike something before the worst came; and as usual it was you who had to run across it. But how are we going to leave our floating home while we pay this week's visit to the plantation of Mr. Buckleyl"

"I thought of that when he said you must come, too, and when I spoke of it to him he told me of a man he knew living on the river—that's his shanty you see below there, with the chimney on the outside—who would look after the boat and Dixie for a dollar and be glad of the chance. It's all fixed, my boy, and you needn't worry a bit. We'll be sure of our grub for a week, see something of a simon-true Southern plantation, earn twenty dollars between us, and get in great shape for business. Say, is it all right?"

Maurice, of course, declared that it was, and thereupon Thad did one of his regular hornpipes, to the amusement of some darkies on the shore, who began mocking him, but in a way that did not give offense.

So that night they made arrangement with the man Mr. Buckley recommended to have him keep their boat in his care, along with the yellow dog.

In the morning they again bade farewell to their comfortable floating home for a brief time, and meeting the planter, joined him in a ride to the interior where his plantation was located.

Mr. Simon Buckley was a character very interesting to Maurice.

He had been something of a soldier of fortune since the Civil War and drifted pretty much around the whole world, so that he was a walking encyclopedia of knowledge upon almost any subject.

What interested Maurice most of all was his association with Uncle Ambrose in Cuba many years before. It was with considerable surprise that the lad learned how his steady-going relative had once upon a time been a wild blade, an adventurer as it were, ready to take up with anything that promised excitement, and a hope of gain in a fairly decent way.

Simon Buckley had been very fond of Anthony, it would seem, and his delight at running across a nephew of his old comrade was unmistakable.

The voyagers had never met with a luckier bit of fortune than when Thad chanced to interview this veteran.

Mr. Buckley had long ago settled down to a humdrum life as a planter, having wedded the daughter of a big man in the parish. When the old spirit of turbulence grew too strong within him to resist lie had to work it off by a bear hunt in the Mississippi canebrakes, or perhaps a lynching bee—he did not state this latter positively, but there was something in the wink he gave the boys while speaking of such things that told them the truth.

They were too wise to think of starting an argument with a Southern man upon a subject of which they had a very small amount of information, and which entered upon his daily life, so they said nothing while he was present.

That ride was one long to be remembered, for they saw things that might never have come under their observation otherwise.

Various plantations were passed, and collections of negro cabins, around which hosts of youngsters were playing, as free from care as the rabbit that ran across the road—indeed, much more so, for Bunny had to look sharp lest he afford a meal for one of his many enemies, while these pickaninnies had their daily wants supplied, and grew up like so many puppies.

Along about noon they reached their destination.

The Buckley plantation was well known in that section as one of the best in western Mississippi.

Of course, the main staple was cotton, king of the South; but there were various other products that the owner raised. He had a grinding mill and produced a large amount of sugar and molasses in season. Then on some lowlands he grew rice of a superior quality. His ambition being to constantly improve on what had been produced the preceding season, his experience all over the world proved of value to him now, when he could calmly review what he had seen and profit by it.

The place seemed an ideal Southern plantation to Maurice, and he soon wished he had a camera along with which to secure some views that he could carry with him wherever he went. As the owner had a weakness that way, the want was supplied before they had been there two days, and when the tune came to depart, lo, Maurice had a dozen or two pictures in his possession to show "Old Ambrose," as the planter said.

Indeed, it took Maurice just two days to straighten the books out, and then Mr. Buckley kept him busy with that camera; for he had had miserable success himself in handling it, and was just hoping some one would come along with a better knowledge of such things than himself.

St. George Rathborne

CHAPTER XXI

A NIGHT HUNT FOR COONS

"What do you think," said Thad, one afternoon, after they had been nearly a week at the plantation, "tonight the major's going to take us out on a regular old 'coon hunt. I've tried to get 'coons that way lots of times up home, but never had the right kind of dog. But that yellow Spider of his is the best in the county, he says, while Crusoe is a good second."

"That sounds fine, and I sure will be glad to go along. But is it Robinson Crusoe he means when he calls that poor white dub?" asked Maurice, looking up from the book he was reading after work hours.

"Yes; you see he found the poor chap with a broken leg on an island in the swamp. He would have starved to death only Mr. Buckley happened along in a canoe. And so he named him Crusoe. They make a splendid pair for the business, he says," went on the excited Thad.

"Who says—Crusoe?" asked the other. "Oh, shucks! You know I mean the major. Now, there's his bear dogs, they're a different proposition, eh; all of 'em big and fierce, just like you'd expect to find when it comes to stopping a black bear in the canebrake. And he says we might try a chance with him tomorrow after Bruin. He's got a rifle to loan us apiece!"

"I suppose you mean the major has, and not the bear. All right, I'm in anything like that. Never saw a wild bear in my life, and perhaps I'll be so scared that I won't know which end of the gun to aim at him; but I'm game to try, Thad; just let him give me a chance."

"Here he comes now," declared Thad.

"Good gracious! the bear?" cried his chum, in pretended alarm.

"Rats! Major Buckley, of course."

The planter was never tired of the company of the two boys. He had no children of his own and enjoyed the coming of these two bright lads so much that he declared it was quite a revelation to him.

"I don't see how I'm going to stand it after you leave here, boys, he said, as he came up; "I never before realized what it meant to have young blood around. Tell you what I proposed to the missus last night after you went to bed. I've got some nephews and nieces down in Natchez, children of my younger brother, Larry. Don't believe they're getting along as well as they might since poor Larry lost his life while out duck hunting in a bayou four years back. I'm thinking seriously of running down to see my kith and kin, and, if I fancy 'em as much as I think I will from the pictures they sent me awhile back, I'm going to bring 'em here, bag and baggage, to make their home with us. And that's what comes of knowing you two lads. They'll have to thank you for their good fortune."

"But we never even heard of them, major," protested Maurice.

"That's so, my lad, but you've made such an impression on my old heart that my eyes are opened, and I see it isn't right for us to live on in this fine place while poor old Larry's children and widow are possibly in want. My mind is quite made up on that score, and if they don't come it won't be my fault," the planter went on.

"Then I'm glad for one that we visited your plantation," asserted Maurice.

"Here, too," echoed his chum, immediately.

Then they fell to talking of the anticipated night's sport with the 'coon pack in the woods.

"It's late for the best hunting in that line," remarked the owner of Crusoe and Spider; "you see the 'coons are fattest along about the ripe corn full moon, and that's when we go after 'em most. Still, I reckon we can scare up a few, though our way of finding 'em may be off color a bit. But I thought you wouldn't mind that, so long as you saw how it was done."

Both boys immediately declared that they were indebted to him for thinking so much about their pleasure.

"Humbug!" said the gentleman, vigorously; "why, your coming has given me more pleasure than I could ever return. It's wakened me up, my wife says, and given me a new lease of life. Why, just to meet one of old Ambrose's nephews has been a tonic for me. Haven't I spent nearly every evening in retailing old stories of our doings over on that blessed island of Cuba, when we were with the insurrectos and fighting against the power of Spain? No, I just couldn't do too much for such fine lads as you are."

Such talk was enough to make both boys blush. But they were growing to like Major Buckley more and more with each passing day, and the recollection of their delightful experiences while his guests would always remain as a happy era in their southward voyage.

"No use going out right after supper, boys. Better wait a little. It's true that the half moon will have about set by then, but we can use torches just as well. Besides, I always think they add to the picturesque character of the hunt. I've had them all prepared of pitch pine, full of resin, and able to give us all the light we want."

Of course, both boys knew considerable about 'coon hunting at night—they would not have been true sons of old Kentucky otherwise. But it happened that neither had ever been fortunate enough to participate in a genuine chase, and the chance appealed to them vigorously.

About nine o'clock the major announced that it was time to make a start.

The barking of the eager dogs that scented the coming fun told that time was passing slowly for them as well. Soon the little party had assembled and started for the edge of the big cornfield. Here several shocks of the white corn had been left as a tempting bait for a late hunt, and it was at such a point they anticipated having the dogs pick up the scent.

Besides the major and the boys there were three colored brothers. One of these was named Black Joe, and he was a faithful old white- headed negro, who had served the major's father through the civil war. When Buckley married and settled down, Ms first act had been to hunt up old Joe and bring him to his plantation as a sort of major-domo or general overseer, and Joe made good every time.

St. George Rathborne

He was a quaint darky, with a fund of original observations that sometimes made it hard for the boys to keep straight faces. Besides, this Black Joe could quote Scripture by the yard, and nothing ever happened but what he had a verse ready. Why, one day when Thad was walking with him over some newly cleared ground, old Joe suddenly clutched his arm, drawing him back and pointing to a little but ugly ground adder that lay in the path, instantly said:

"Man mus' watch as well as pray!"

And no one could manage the 'coon pack as well as Black Joe. When the excitement raged, and the best trained dogs were frantic, the master might command without obtaining obedience; but let old Joe tell a dog to stop barking, or to get out of sight, and it was simply wonderful how his words bore fruit.

A trail was immediately struck by the first shock of corn— this was the flint variety, and as such generally used for hominy throughout the entire south.

Away went the pack with a chorus of eager yelps, while the hunters trailed after them.

"No hurry, boys," said the major, leisurely; "when they get him treed they'll let us know. Then's the time for us to get near and decide whether the tree shall be chopped or a nigger climb up to knock the critter down to the dogs. We never shoot a 'coon 'less the dogs prove unable to master him."

"Then that does sometimes happen, sir?" questioned Thad.

"Occasionally, but not often. A big 'coon may have unusually sharp claws and tear the dogs bad. Then he jumps another tree before they can stop him. After that we think it best to knock him down, rather than risk the lives of the dogs. They's plenty of 'coons, you see, but mighty few good dogs,"

Maurice smiled at the sentiment expressed, and yet it covered the ground from the standpoint of the man. The 'coon's opinion was not worth asking, it seemed.

Suddenly the yelping changed its tenor.

"Does that mean that the 'coon has got away?" asked Maurice.

"Not by a jug full. He's taken to a tree. I reckon they hit it up so fast after him he couldn't reach his own tree, so he bounced up the nearest one. We'll soon see," said the major, as they moved in the direction of the clamor.

"What if he gets to his home tree?" continued Thad, who wanted to know it all, even though not from Missouri.

"That we call good luck, because, you see, boys, sometimes we get three or four varmints out of the one stand. Why, I remember once we kept smoking 'em out till nine had been shook by the dogs. It was what I called the colony tree," laughed the planter.

Presently they drew close to the spot where the racket was being maintained by the dogs. The 'coon was silent, but doubtless his eyes glowed maliciously as he squatted on a limb or in'a fork and surveyed the yelping crew below.

"I sees 'im!" exclaimed one of the negroes, pointing upward, 'right on dat 'ere limb nigh whar it fo'ks, sah. Dat Mistah Coon, foh suah, 'deed it am!" exclaimed the discoverer.

"You're right, Klem," said the major, upon looking closely; "see, boys, you can detect the yellow gleam of his eyes as he watches us; but not a blessed movement does he make. Hey, Klem, you saw him first, and it's your chance to climb up and knock him out."

The negro hardly waited for permission, knowing the rules under which his master usually hunted at night. He had a club in his hand, which he transferred to his teeth as he started to climb.

The tree was rather large and would have taken too much time to fell for one coon; so another method was resorted to in order to get the animal down to where the eager dogs could pounce upon him.

"Look at the dogs!" said Maurice to his chum, while the climber was cautiously approaching the animal on the limb, so as to prevent it from ascending higher into the tree.

They were almost frantic, licking their chops, whining and actually shivering with eagerness. Well did they know that presently there would come to the ground a furry mass with sharp claws and teeth, on which they were expected to leap and finish with a few bites directed either at the throat or the backbone.

"Watch out dar!" came in a thrilling tone from above.

Klem was now close upon the coon, which had retreated further out on the limb. When the negro climber had gone as far as he dared he suddenly gave a shake that sent the wretched animal in a struggling heap down through space.

The dogs were waiting. They saw the coon coming and were on the spot ere he landed, so that almost before he could attempt any resistance both Crusoe and Spider were at his throat.

There was a short, if furious, tussle, for a coon is gifted with considerable strength and agility, though seldom a match for the right, kind of a dog.

Then it was all over.

The major lifted the still quivering animal.

"Pretty fat critter. A few more like him will pay us for coming out, boys," he declared.

Then they once more returned to the cornfield, where the keen nosed dogs speedily caught up another scent.

Again the party followed leisurely until the signal came that the quarry had been safely treed. This time they found that it was only a small tree, so it was cut down.

"I want you to see all the phases of coon hunting, boys," explained the planter, while the chips were flying under the axes of Klein and Cudjo.

Of course, the instant the swaying tree commenced to topple the animal made a frantic leap; but those sharp eyes of the dogs had never once lost track of the quarry, and they were quickly after the coon, which, unable to scurry up another tree, had to turn at bay.

It was soon over, and a second victim had been added to the score, much to the delight of the blacks, who knew they would surely have their share of the spoils of the night hunt.

The next coon turned out to be a fat 'possum, and loud were

St. George Rathborne

the exclamations of joy on the part of Klem and his comrades when this fact was made plain. Indeed, Maurice believed he would not have taken any great stock in this method of hunting, which seemed so unfair to the game, only on account of the chances it gave the negroes for a square meal in the line of the greatest delicacies they knew. So the hunt went on for several hours.

When about midnight they concluded to return to the house, seven coons and two 'possums were loaded upon the shoulders of the three attendants. And the dogs lagged behind, quite tired out with their exertions; though ready to prick up their ears at ike slightest suspicious sound from the gloomy woods around them.

"How did you like it, Maurice," asked Thad later on, as they were getting ready for bed.

"Oh, it was an interesting experience," returned the other; "but I don't know that I'd give much to repeat the dose."

And Thad was of the same mind. "But that bear hunt will be something different, you bet," he observed.

It was.

CHAPTER XXII

SHIPMATES FOR A ROUND THE WORLD CRUISE

Each passing day presented some new and attractive feature along the banks of the great river; and under other conditions Maurice would have been delighted to go ashore and witness the operation of grinding sugarcane, or baling cotton where the cotton gin worked. But these things would have to keep until another occasion, for destiny now beckoned to the two lads, and they felt that their fortunes were wrapped up in this anticipated meeting with the old sailor.

On the twelfth of February, at two in the afternoon, they arrived at the upper stretch of the river metropolis, and from that time on they kept fully on the alert so as to avoid a collision with some passing boat.

At the same time they were also looking for a certain boatyard, to which they had been recommended by Mr. Buckley, who knew the proprietor well, and for whom a letter was reposing in the pocket of Maurice's coat.

Luckily this boatyard was near the upper part of the city, so that they did not have to pass along the entire water front, in constant danger of a spill from the many vessels moving about, great tows of coal barges such as they had seen on the

St. George Rathborne

river many times, ocean steamers, ferry boats, sailboats and numerous other river craft propelled by steam, gasoline or sails.

The proprietor of the boatyard looked at them a bit suspiciously as they drew the ungainly craft that had served them as a home during the long cruise, into his "pocket;" but upon reading the letter Maurice presented his face changed in its expression and he shook hands with both lads heartily.

And thus early in their experience in the world our boys realized what a splendid thing it is at any and all times to have a friend at court, ready to speak a good work in one's favor.

They could tie up in the yard, and he would see to keeping the shanty-boat with some things aboard, to be given to their friend, Bob Archiable, when he arrived.

And yet Maurice and his friend looked at the Tramp with regret in their eyes when they were saying good-by to the craft; for they had enjoyed many good times aboard the faithful little floating home since leaving the Indiana town, and would have many pleasant memories in the dim future to look back upon.

Mr. Buckley had insisted upon Maurice taking the little snapshot camera along with him when he departed, saying that he had ordered a larger and more expensive one; and that it was worth it to be shown how to develop and print in the clever manner Maurice had done.

So, as there was a roll of film in the camera, Maurice had used it in taking pictures of the boat and Dixie while they were floating downstream; and if these turned out well they would always have a reminder of their staunch craft and the little yellow cur that had helped to brighten the voyage, now given over to the friendly boat builder, who had conceived a fancy for him.

But that night they spent in their old quarters, getting things in shape for a move in the morning, when they expected to find some boarding place where they could put up until the arrival of the Campertown.

It was one of the worst nights of the trip, for the sounds that came to them from the city streets were so strange to their ears that, as Thad declared, they seemed to be near some boiler factory. Of course this was mostly because they had been off by themselves for months, and the night meant a time of solemn silence, save for the murmur of the wind through the trees, or the splash of the waves upon the shore, or against the side of the boat.

When day came both boys felt a bit rocky, having rested wretchedly; but after fixing up and sallying forth they found a restaurant where the demands of the inner man could be satisfied, and then things began to assume a brighter aspect in their eyes.

Maurice purchased a paper and looked up the nautical news to see whether the steamer of his uncle had arrived, or was spoken outside the mouth of the river.

To his delight he discovered that she was expected on the following morning, and during the day he and Thad found their way to the identical spot where the Campertown would be apt to lay up when releasing her cargo and taking on another.

They spent the better part of the day in seeing the city, now in holiday attire, for it was the last of the Mardi Gras festivities, as Lent was close at hand.

That night was a banner one to the two lads, who had never been in a great city before, and especially at a time when the whole population seemed to have given itself up to gaiety.

They spent the time upon the streets until past midnight, watching the floats go by in gorgeous procession, and mixing up with the festive maskers bent upon having all the fun possible, since tomorrow they must begin to mourn.

Thoroughly tired out, our boys finally said good-by to these riotous sounds and hied away to the quiet house where they had a room. Once abed there was no need on this night to toss and turn, for they hardly hit the pillow before they lost all track of time and were sound asleep.

Another dawn found them up and eager to get down to the river.

They could hardly wait to get their breakfast before putting out at full speed.

The steamer had come in during the night, and with emotions that would be indeed difficult to define they read the word Campertown.

How big she looked to them—for they had never seen anything larger than a river steamboat until the preceding day; and to think that this palatial vessel (for such the tramp appeared in their eyes) might be their home for months, yes, years to come.

Maurice boldly asked for the captain, and was told that he was asleep, and on no condition could he be seen until ten; so they had to content themselves with wandering around and talking about what the chances were for success.

Thad was very nervous, for it must be understood that as yet good Uncle Ambrose did not even know that such a fellow existed on earth, and his future was, to say the least, uncertain.

The possibility of being separated by a cruel fate from this chum whom he loved so well was beginning to give Thad a heartache; and his hands trembled in spite of his smiling face, every time he looked at Maurice.

The time that elapsed until the hour of ten arrived was about as weary a stretch as either of our lads ever knew; indeed, Thad afterward declared that it was worse than on the occasion when they had to put in an hour of dreadful suspense in the cabin of the shanty-boat while the storm raged on the river, and it was doubtful whether they would ever see daylight again.

But finally the time came for them to go aboard; and mustering their courage to the fore they went up the gang plank.

A sailor directed them to the captain's room and here Maurice discovered a big man in a uniform, whose bearded face had a kindly look, and who at his entrance jumped up, stared at him a couple of seconds and then pounced upon him like a great grizzly bear, grasping both his hands and roaring:

"Jim's boy for all the world—he very image of his dad as I remember him, I'm mighty glad to see you, Maurice, and at first sight I know we're going to get on fine together. And you're come down to go with old Uncle Ambrose to foreign ports, eh? That's great. I tell you this does me good, just to see you, lad. I've been getting kind of homesick lately—ought to have been ashamed of myself for not looking you up sooner; but a fellow who's in all parts of the world loses his grip on things sometimes; but never mind, I'm going to make it up to you from now on. But who's this with you, son?"

That made the desired opening; so Thad was introduced as the finest fellow in all the world, and before Maurice knew it he had launched out on a narrative of their long cruise down the great river, in which Thad had borne himself as a true American boy should, always ready to take his turn at duty, never shirking peril or stress, and cooking the most delightful meals that anybody ever ate.

Captain Haddon's eyes gleamed with humor as he heard the virtues of the modest Thad thus extolled to the skies; he knew what was coming, but it pleased him to keep the boys on the anxious seat a while, for this was a every amusing happening to the old salt.

And then, when they told how they had spent a week and more with his old "bunky" Simon Buckley, he was intensely interested; whereupon Maurice saw fit to bring out the letter of recommendation wherein the said Simon declared that Thad was certainly a good, conscientious carpenter, and he could wager his old friend would never regret it if he saw fit to give the lad a chance on board his vessel.

Then the captain looked at Thad, sizing him up from the crown of his head to his toes, after which he thrust out his hand and said heartily:

"Tip us your fin, Thad, my lad. It would be cruelty to separate two such good shanty-boat mates as you. I'll find something for you to do aboard, and by thunder you'll see the world together. That cruise was immense, and I'd have enjoyed nothing better myself than to have been along with you. I expect to hear many a yarn concerning those happenings as we sail across the big pond; for our next port call is going to be Liverpool, where we take on a cargo for Australia, and then to Japan, so you see before you're a year older both of you may have gone almost around the world; for we're likely to bring up at 'Frisco. Thad, consider that you're as good as booked for the trip. And now go about your business for a time. Here, Maurice, take this little amount for expenses, and be back on board by evening. Tomorrow I'll start you in at your work under my present man, who is quitting us by the time we leave Orleans."

Maurice could hardly find words to thank him, and Thad was in the same boat; but then the old sea-dog understood boys, and he knew just how they felt, so that as each of them shook hands with him and looked mutely in his face he only grinned and nodded and said:

"I know all about it, lads, how you feel. But you've made me happier than you are yourselves. I was beginning to get into a rut, and seemed to have nothing to live for. The sight of you, my boy, has made me ten years younger. Bun along now, and don't get into any mischief; but I can see with one eye that neither of you have any use for grog, and there's little chance for trouble when that is avoided."

They went ashore with light hearts; indeed, it seemed as though they must be treading on air, and they could hardly refrain from hugging each other, the world looked so bright in their eyes.

It was a ten dollar bill the rugged old captain had thrust into the hand of Maurice; and one of the first things he did was to go to a photographer and have some prints made of the films

St. George Rathborne

exposed during the latter part of the voyage; for already he was feeling some signs of homesickness in connection with the poor old Tramp, and desirous of showing his uncle what a "bully old floater" she was, as Thad said.

What they did not do the balance of the day would be easier to tell than any attempt to describe the many things they saw and experienced; but taken in all it was a red letter time, never to be forgotten.

The future beckoned with enticing fingers, and the horizon looked red with the glowing promise of hope; but at the same time as they glanced backward they would always have tender feelings for every memory connected with that river trip, and the shanty-boat on which the voyage had been made.

THE END

Choose from Thousands of 1stWorldLibrary Classics By

A. M. Barnard	Booth Tarkington	Edward Everett Hale
Ada Leverson	Boyd Cable	Edward J. O'Biren
Adolphus William Ward	Bram Stoker	Edward S. Ellis
Aesop	C. Collodi	Edwin L. Arnold
Agatha Christie	C. E. Orr	Eleanor Atkins
Alexander Aaronsohn	C. M. Ingleby	Eleanor Hallowell Abbott
Alexander Kielland	Carolyn Wells	Eliot Gregory
Alexandre Dumas	Catherine Parr Traill	Elizabeth Gaskell
Alfred Gatty	Charles A. Eastman	Elizabeth McCracken
Alfred Ollivant	Charles Amory Beach	Elizabeth Von Arnim
Alice Duer Miller	Charles Dickens	Ellem Key
Alice Turner Curtis	Charles Dudley Warner	Emerson Hough
Alice Dunbar	Charles Farrar Browne	Emilie F. Carlen
Allen Chapman	Charles Ives	Emily Bronte
Alleyne Ireland	Charles Kingsley	Emily Dickinson
Ambrose Bierce	Charles Klein	Enid Bagnold
Amelia E. Barr	Charles Hanson Towne	Enilor Macartney Lane
Amory H. Bradford	Charles Lathrop Pack	Erasmus W. Jones
Andrew Lang	Charles Romyn Dake	Ernie Howard Pie
Andrew McFarland Davis	Charles Whibley	Ethel May Dell
Andy Adams	Charles Willing Beale	Ethel Turner
Angela Brazil	Charlotte M. Braeme	Ethel Watts Mumford
Anna Alice Chapin	Charlotte M. Yonge	Eugene Sue
Anna Sewell	Charlotte Perkins Stetson	Eugenie Foa
Annie Besant	Clair W. Hayes	Eugene Wood
Annie Hamilton Donnell	Clarence Day Jr.	Eustace Hale Ball
Annie Payson Call	Clarence E. Mulford	Evelyn Everett-green
Annie Roe Carr	Clemence Housman	Everard Cotes
Annonaymous	Confucius	F. H. Cheley
Anton Chekhov	Coningsby Dawson	F. J. Cross
Archibald Lee Fletcher	Cornelis DeWitt Wilcox	F. Marion Crawford
Arnold Bennett	Cyril Burleigh	Fannie E. Newberry
Arthur C. Benson	D. H. Lawrence	Federick Austin Ogg
Arthur Conan Doyle	Daniel Defoe	Ferdinand Ossendowski
Arthur M. Winfield	David Garnett	Fergus Hume
Arthur Ransome	Dinah Craik	Florence A. Kilpatrick
Arthur Schnitzler	Don Carlos Janes	Fremont B. Deering
Arthur Train	Donald Keyhoe	Francis Bacon
Atticus	Dorothy Kilner	Francis Darwin
B.H. Baden-Powell	Dougan Clark	Frances Hodgson Burnett
B. M. Bower	Douglas Fairbanks	Frances Parkinson Keyes
B. C. Chatterjee	E. Nesbit	Frank Gee Patchin
Baroness Emmuska Orczy	E. P. Roe	Frank Harris
Baroness Orczy	E. Phillips Oppenheim	Frank Jewett Mather
Basil King	E. S. Brooks	Frank L. Packard
Bayard Taylor	Earl Barnes	Frank V. Webster
Ben Macomber	Edgar Rice Burroughs	Frederic Stewart Isham
Bertha Muzzy Bower	Edith Van Dyne	Frederick Trevor Hill
Bjornstjerne Bjornson	Edith Wharton	Frederick Winslow Taylor

Friedrich Kerst
Friedrich Nietzsche
Fyodor Dostoyevsky
G.A. Henty
G.K. Chesterton
Gabrielle E. Jackson
Garrett P. Serviss
Gaston Leroux
George A. Warren
George Ade
Geroge Bernard Shaw
George Cary Eggleston
George Durston
George Ebers
George Eliot
George Gissing
George MacDonald
George Meredith
George Orwell
George Sylvester Viereck
George Tucker
George W. Cable
George Wharton James
Gertrude Atherton
Gordon Casserly
Grace E. King
Grace Gallatin
Grace Greenwood
Grant Allen
Guillermo A. Sherwell
Gulielma Zollinger
Gustav Flaubert
H. A. Cody
H. B. Irving
H. C. Bailey
H. G. Wells
H. H. Munro
H. Irving Hancock
H. R. Naylor
H. Rider Haggard
H. W. C. Davis
Haldeman Julius
Hall Caine
Hamilton Wright Mabie
Hans Christian Andersen
Harold Avery
Harold McGrath
Harriet Beecher Stowe
Harry Castlemon
Harry Coghill
Harry Houidini

Hayden Carruth
Helent Hunt Jackson
Helen Nicolay
Hendrik Conscience
Hendy David Thoreau
Henri Barbusse
Henrik Ibsen
Henry Adams
Henry Ford
Henry Frost
Henry James
Henry Jones Ford
Henry Seton Merriman
Henry W Longfellow
Herbert A. Giles
Herbert Carter
Herbert N. Casson
Herman Hesse
Hildegard G. Frey
Homer
Honore De Balzac
Horace B. Day
Horace Walpole
Horatio Alger Jr.
Howard Pyle
Howard R. Garis
Hugh Lofting
Hugh Walpole
Humphry Ward
Ian Maclaren
Inez Haynes Gillmore
Irving Bacheller
Isabel Cecilia Williams
Isabel Hornibrook
Israel Abrahams
Ivan Turgenev
J. G.Austin
J. Henri Fabre
J. M. Barrie
J. M. Walsh
J. Macdonald Oxley
J. R. Miller
J. S. Fletcher
J. S. Knowles
J. Storer Clouston
J. W. Duffield
Jack London
Jacob Abbott
James Allen
James Andrews
James Baldwin

James Branch Cabell
James DeMille
James Joyce
James Lane Allen
James Lane Allen
James Oliver Curwood
James Oppenheim
James Otis
James R. Driscoll
Jane Abbott
Jane Austen
Jane L. Stewart
Janet Aldridge
Jens Peter Jacobsen
Jerome K. Jerome
Jessie Graham Flower
John Buchan
John Burroughs
John Cournos
John F. Kennedy
John Gay
John Glasworthy
John Habberton
John Joy Bell
John Kendrick Bangs
John Milton
John Philip Sousa
John Taintor Foote
Jonas Lauritz Idemil Lie
Jonathan Swift
Joseph A. Altsheler
Joseph Carey
Joseph Conrad
Joseph E. Badger Jr
Joseph Hergesheimer
Joseph Jacobs
Jules Vernes
Julian Hawthrone
Julie A Lippmann
Justin Huntly McCarthy
Kakuzo Okakura
Karle Wilson Baker
Kate Chopin
Kenneth Grahame
Kenneth McGaffey
Kate Langley Bosher
Kate Langley Bosher
Katherine Cecil Thurston
Katherine Stokes
L. A. Abbot
L. T. Meade

L. Frank Baum
Latta Griswold
Laura Dent Crane
Laura Lee Hope
Laurence Housman
Lawrence Beasley
Leo Tolstoy
Leonid Andreyev
Lewis Carroll
Lewis Sperry Chafer
Lilian Bell
Lloyd Osbourne
Louis Hughes
Louis Joseph Vance
Louis Tracy
Louisa May Alcott
Lucy Fitch Perkins
Lucy Maud Montgomery
Luther Benson
Lydia Miller Middleton
Lyndon Orr
M. Corvus
M. H. Adams
Margaret E. Sangster
Margret Howth
Margaret Vandercook
Margaret W. Hungerford
Margret Penrose
Maria Edgeworth
Maria Thompson Daviess
Mariano Azuela
Marion Polk Angellotti
Mark Overton
Mark Twain
Mary Austin
Mary Catherine Crowley
Mary Cole
Mary Hastings Bradley
Mary Roberts Rinehart
Mary Rowlandson
M. Wollstonecraft Shelley
Maud Lindsay
Max Beerbohm
Myra Kelly
Nathaniel Hawthrone
Nicolo Machiavelli
O. F. Walton
Oscar Wilde
Owen Johnson
P.G. Wodehouse
Paul and Mabel Thorne

Paul G. Tomlinson
Paul Severing
Percy Brebner
Percy Keese Fitzhugh
Peter B. Kyne
Plato
Quincy Allen
R. Derby Holmes
R. L. Stevenson
R. S. Ball
Rabindranath Tagore
Rahul Alvares
Ralph Bonehill
Ralph Henry Barbour
Ralph Victor
Ralph Waldo Emmerson
Rene Descartes
Ray Cummings
Rex Beach
Rex E. Beach
Richard Harding Davis
Richard Jefferies
Richard Le Gallienne
Robert Barr
Robert Frost
Robert Gordon Anderson
Robert L. Drake
Robert Lansing
Robert Lynd
Robert Michael Ballantyne
Robert W. Chambers
Rosa Nouchette Carey
Rudyard Kipling
Saint Augustine
Samuel B. Allison
Samuel Hopkins Adams
Sarah Bernhardt
Sarah C. Hallowell
Selma Lagerlof
Sherwood Anderson
Sigmund Freud
Standish O'Grady
Stanley Weyman
Stella Benson
Stella M. Francis
Stephen Crane
Stewart Edward White
Stijn Streuvels
Swami Abhedananda
Swami Parmananda
T. S. Ackland

T. S. Arthur
The Princess Der Ling
Thomas A. Janvier
Thomas A Kempis
Thomas Anderton
Thomas Bailey Aldrich
Thomas Bulfinch
Thomas De Quincey
Thomas Dixon
Thomas H. Huxley
Thomas Hardy
Thomas More
Thornton W. Burgess
U. S. Grant
Upton Sinclair
Valentine Williams
Various Authors
Vaughan Kester
Victor Appleton
Victor G. Durham
Victoria Cross
Virginia Woolf
Wadsworth Camp
Walter Camp
Walter Scott
Washington Irving
Wilbur Lawton
Wilkie Collins
Willa Cather
Willard F. Baker
William Dean Howells
William le Queux
W. Makepeace Thackeray
William W. Walter
William Shakespeare
Winston Churchill
Yei Theodora Ozaki
Yogi Ramacharaka
Young E. Allison
Zane Grey